F**k You!
Adult Swear Word Coloring Book 50+ Designs

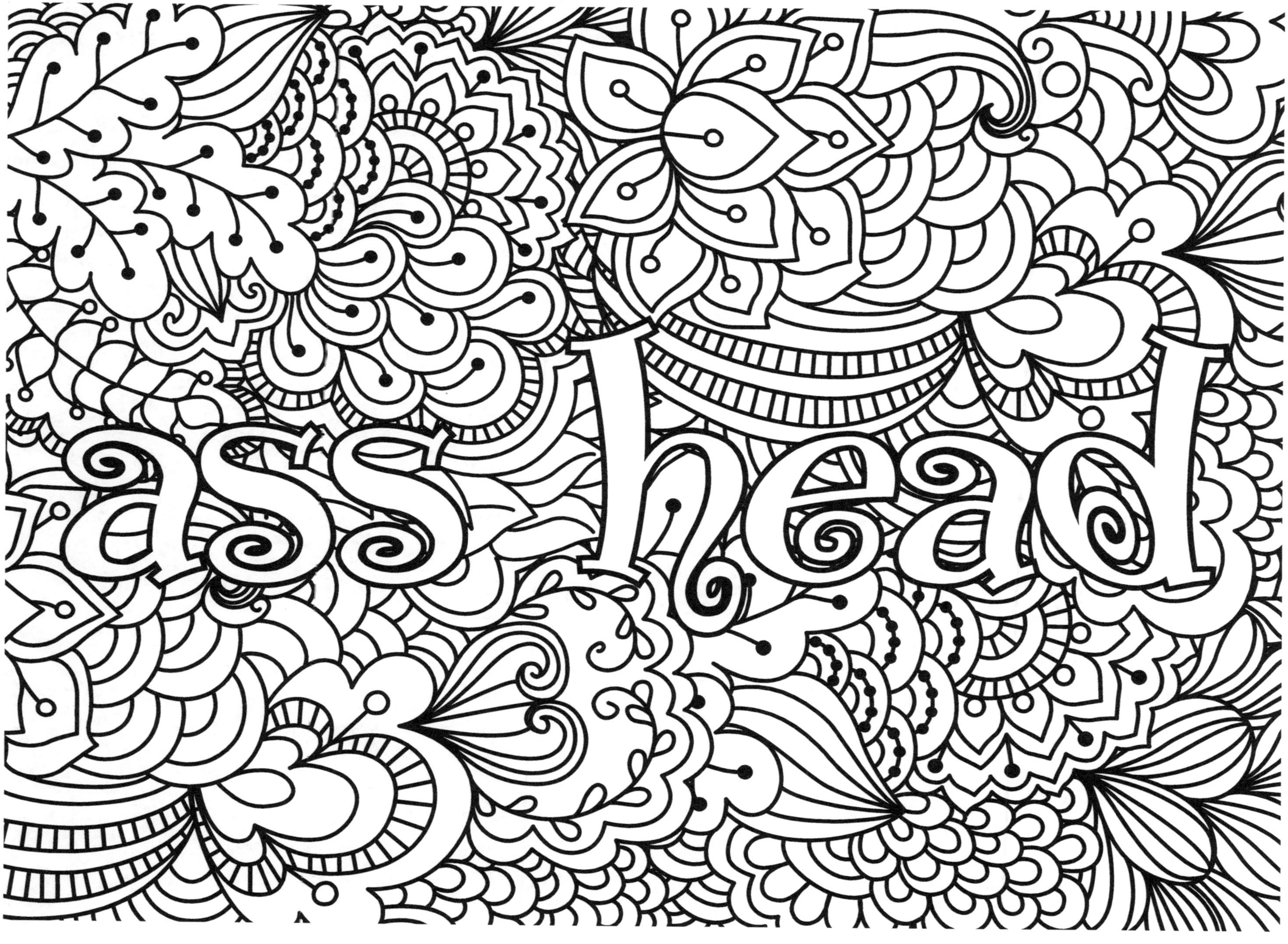
ass head

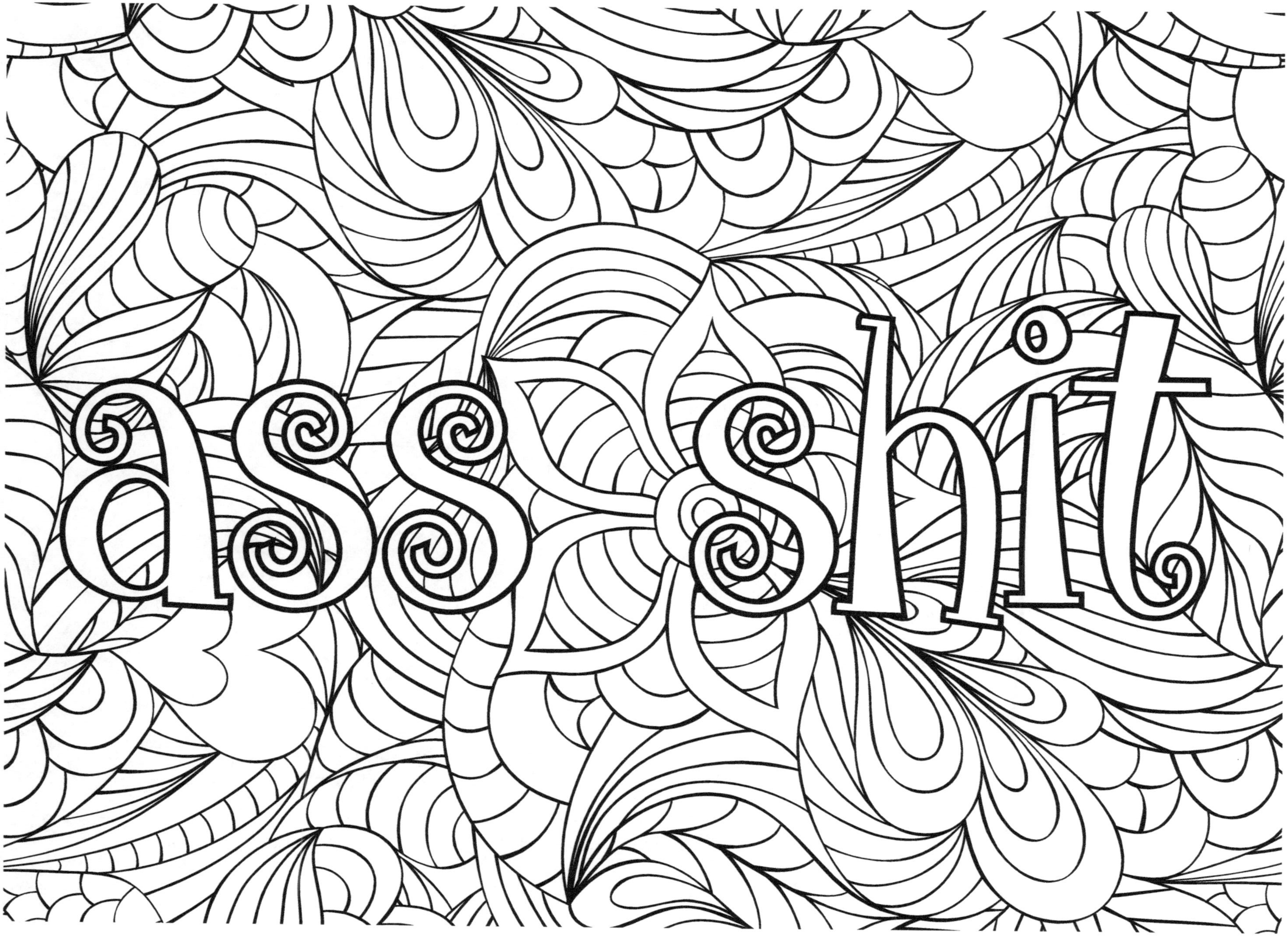
assshit

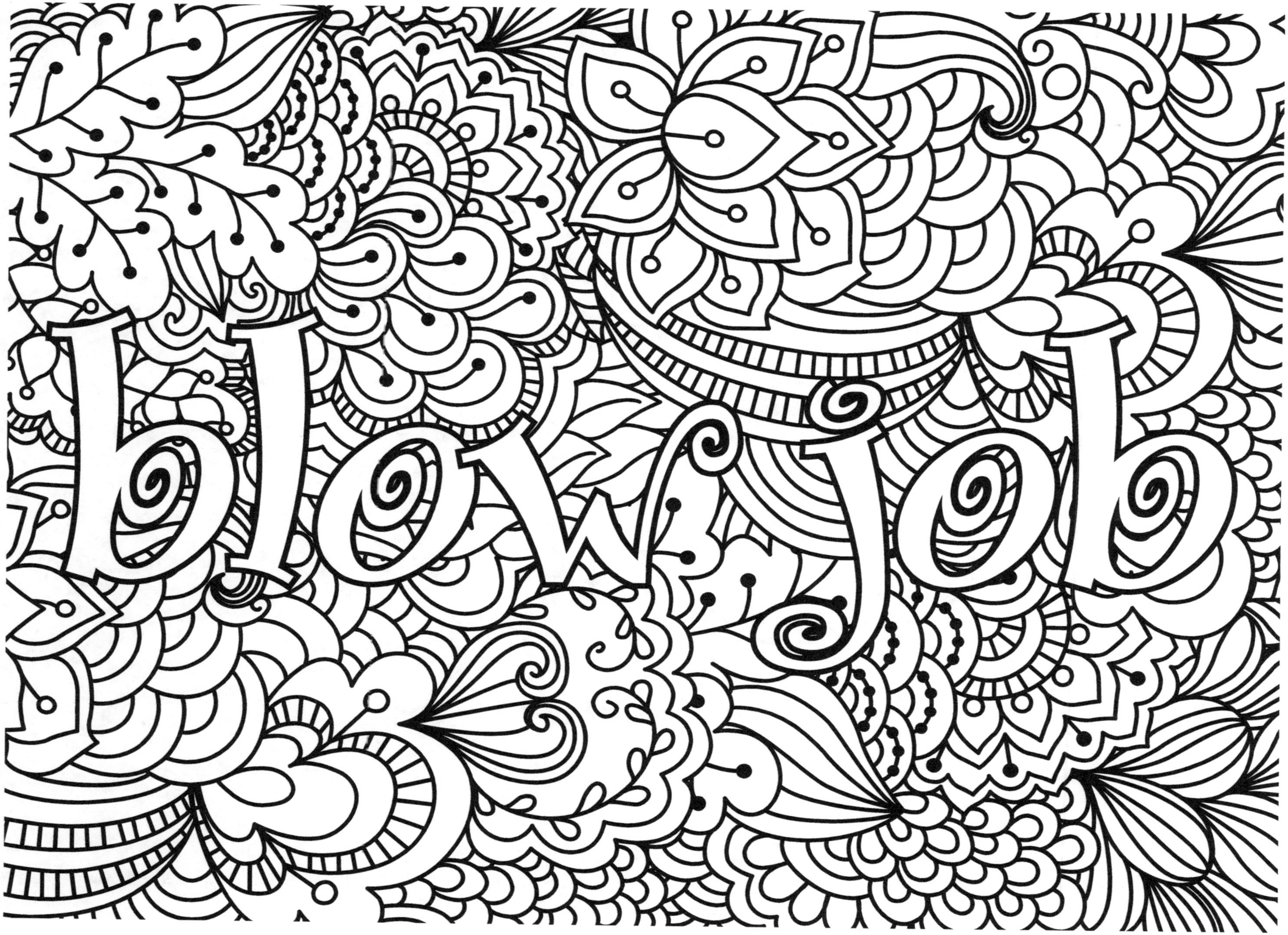
blowjob

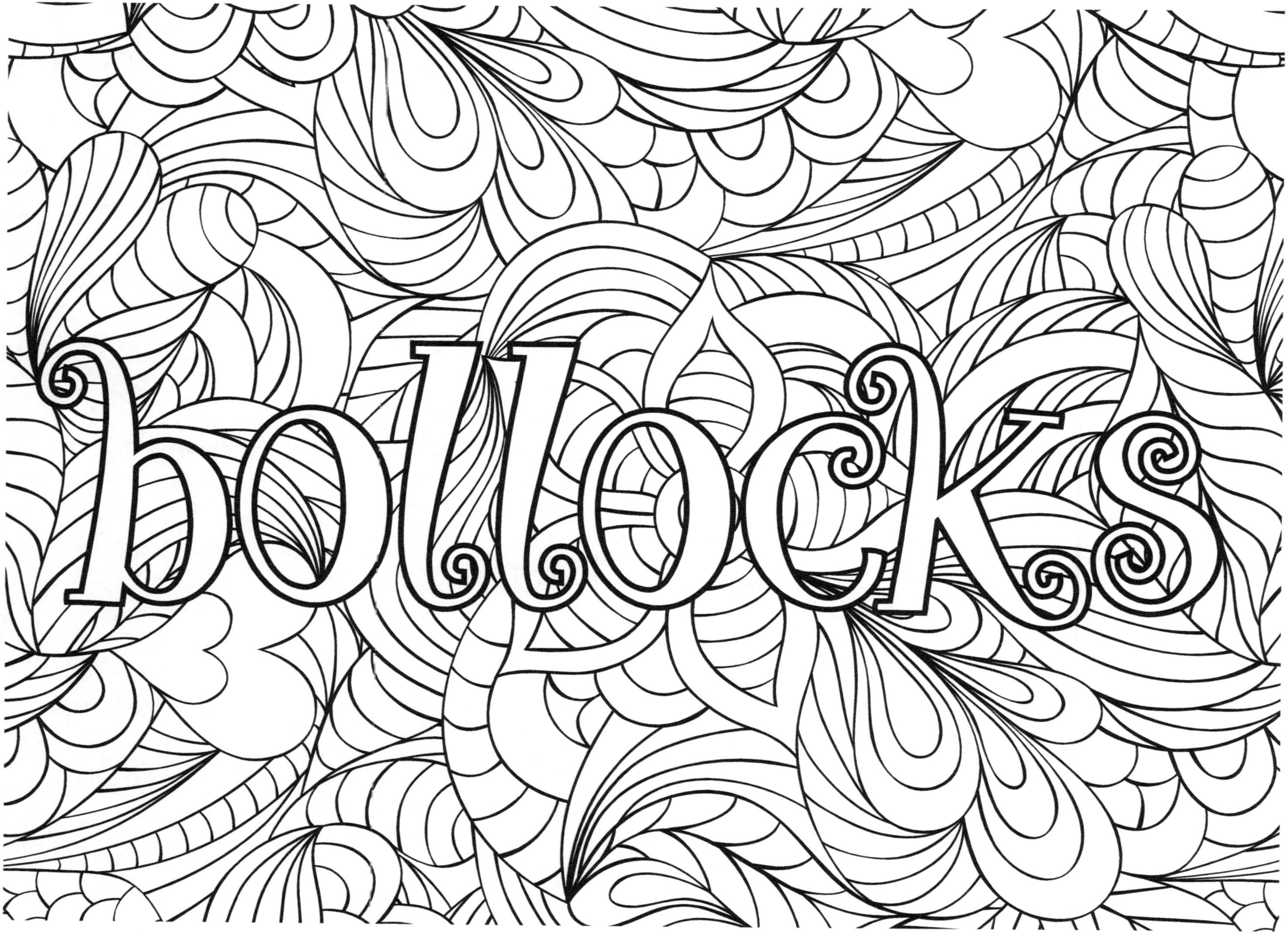
bollocks

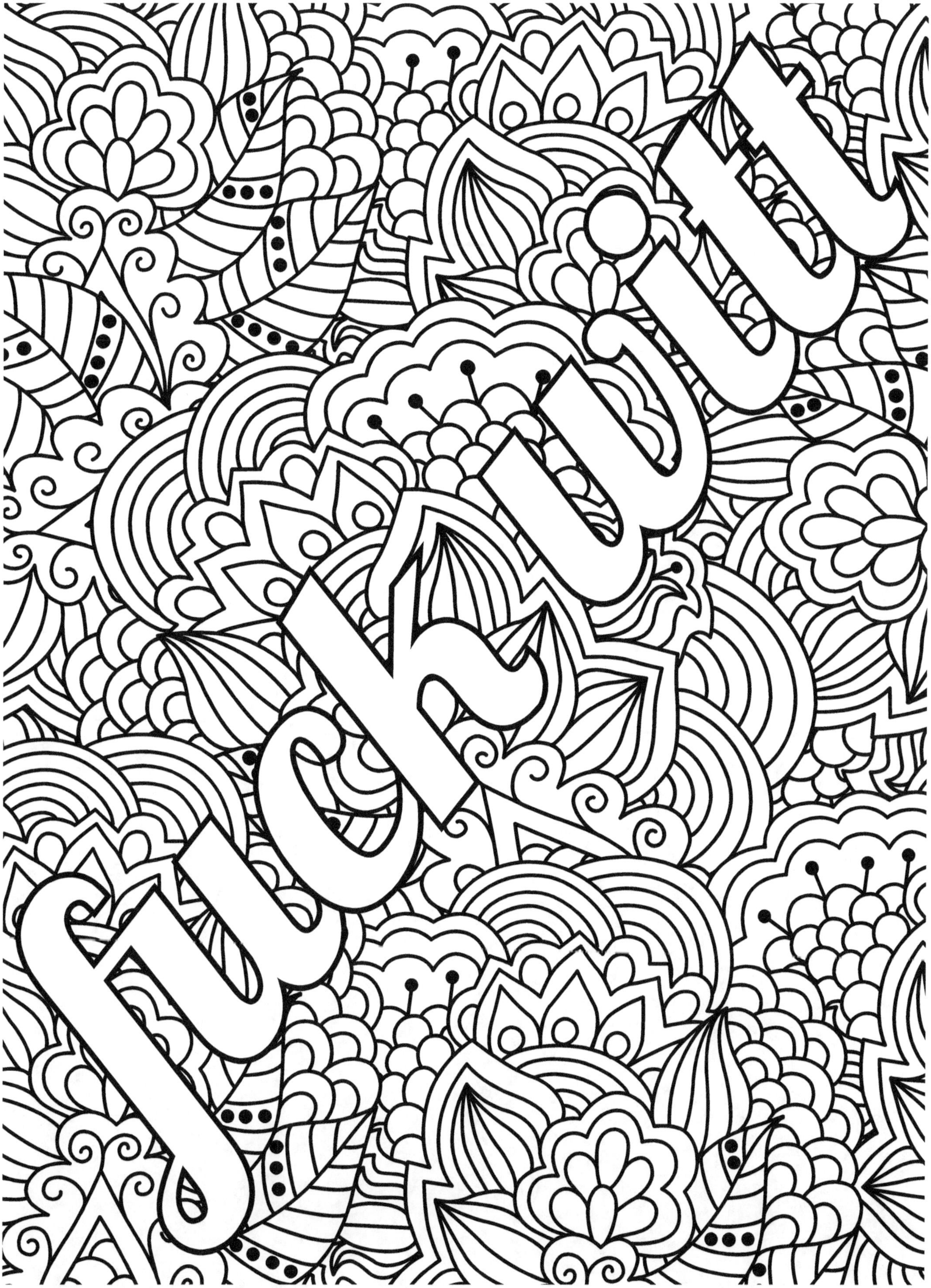
fuckwit

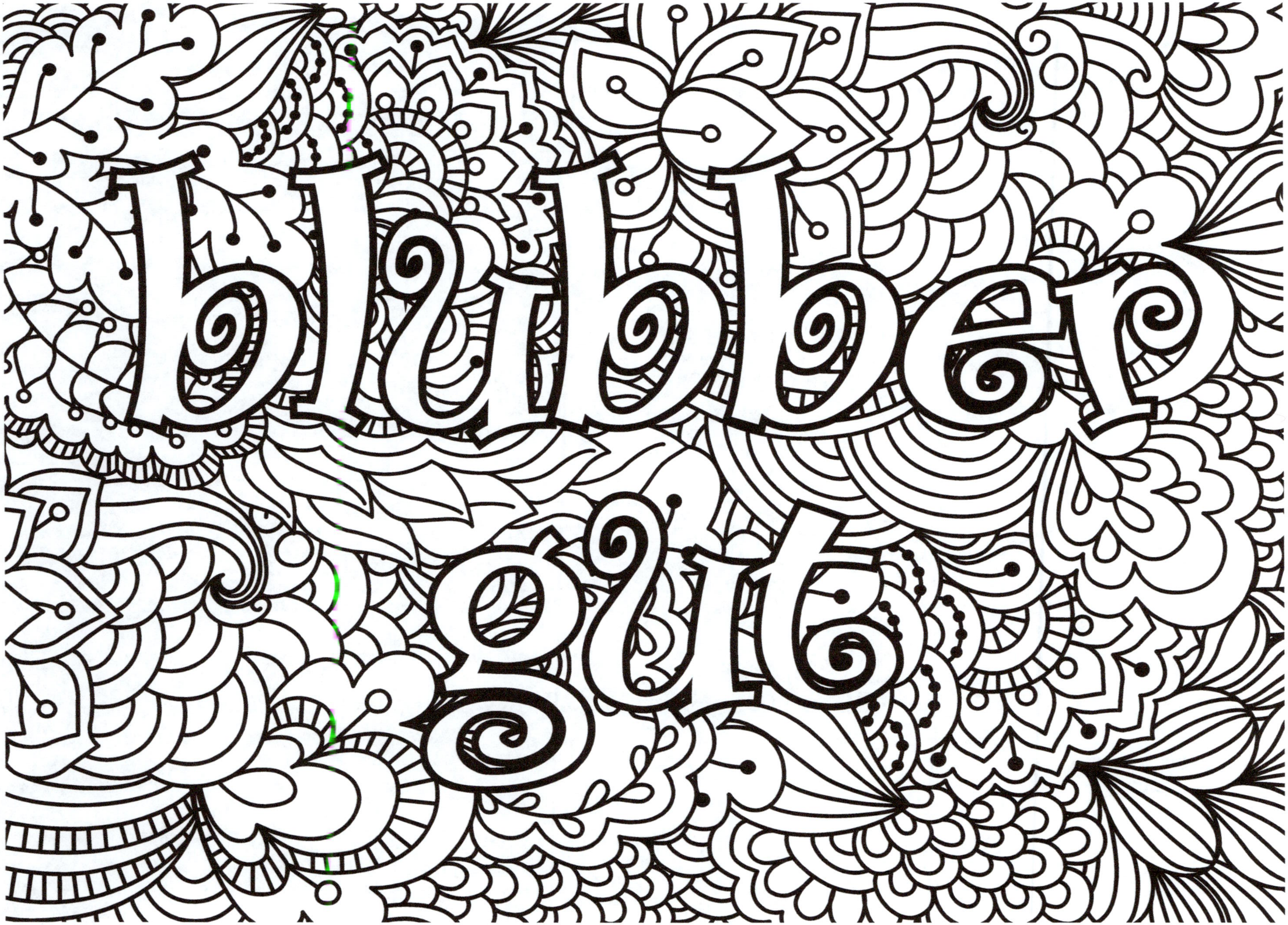
blubber
gut

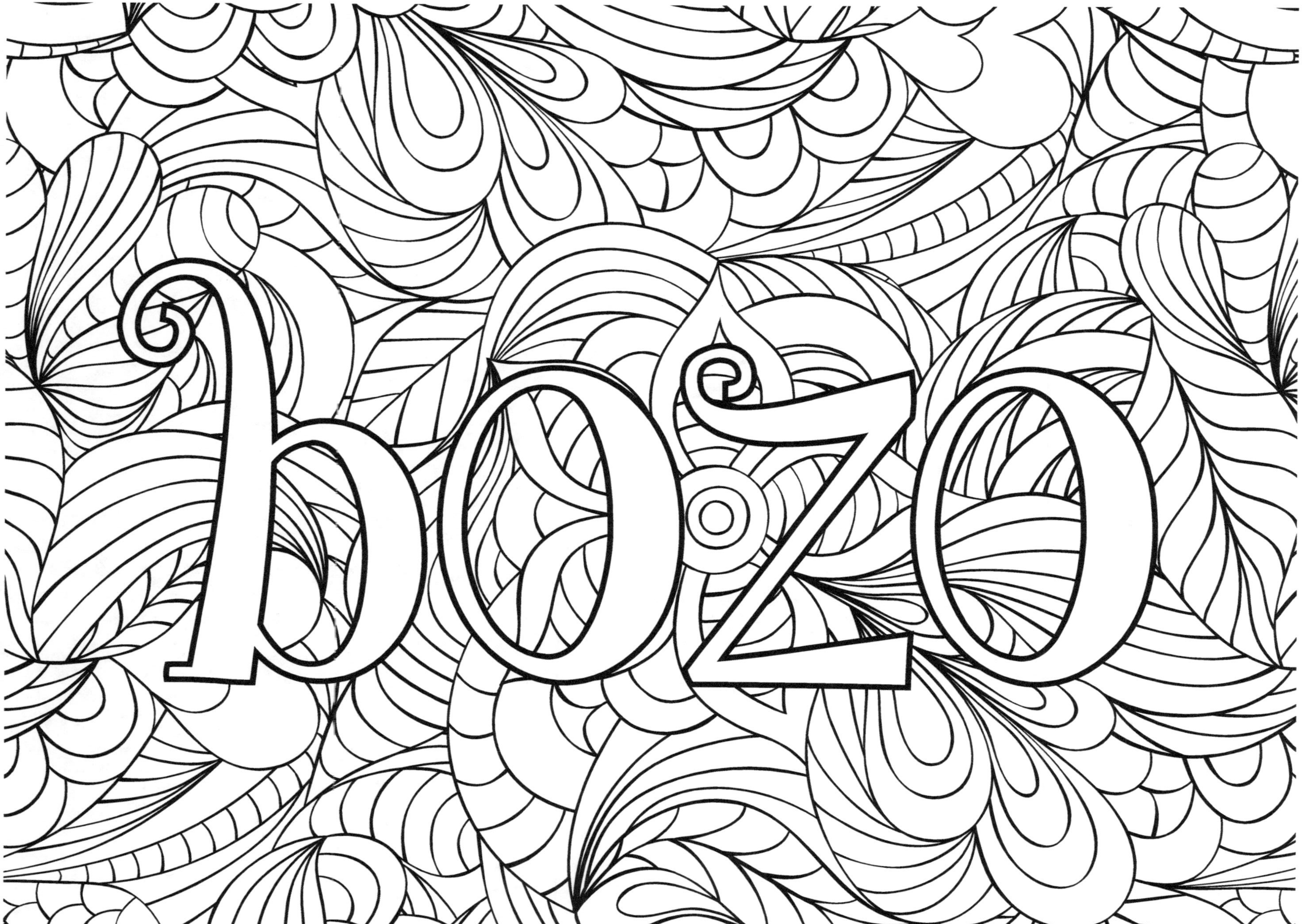
bozo

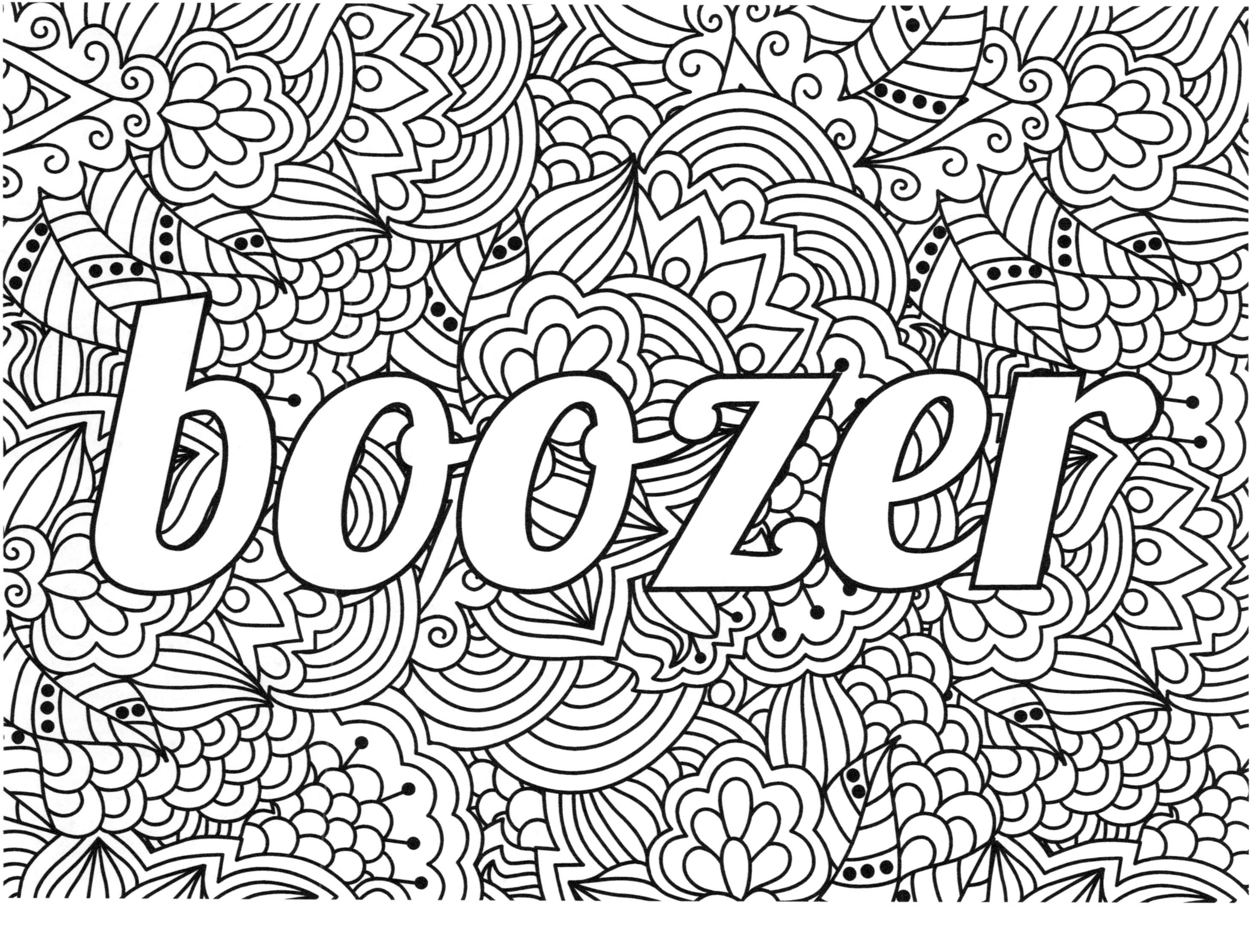
boozer

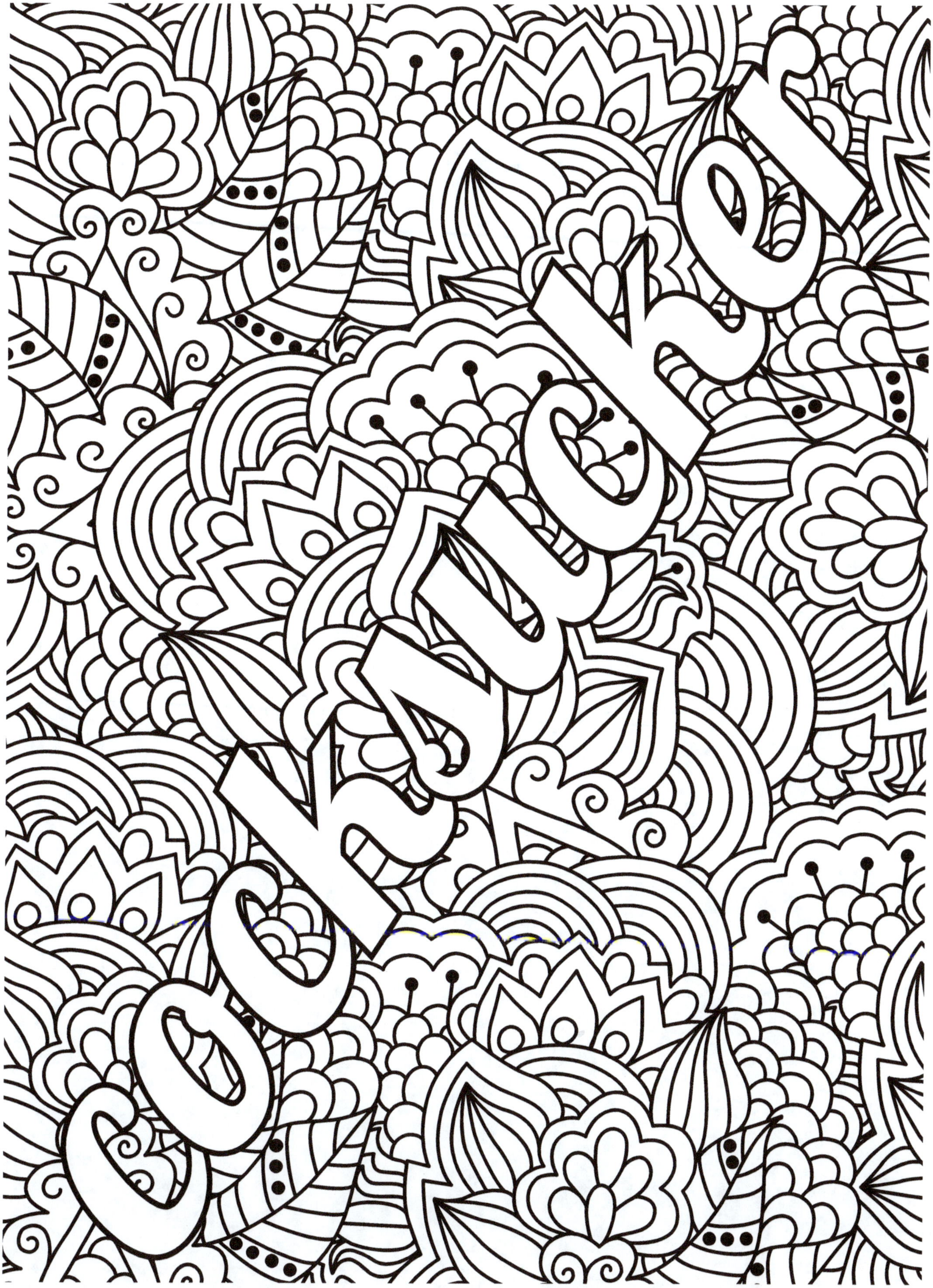
Cocksucker

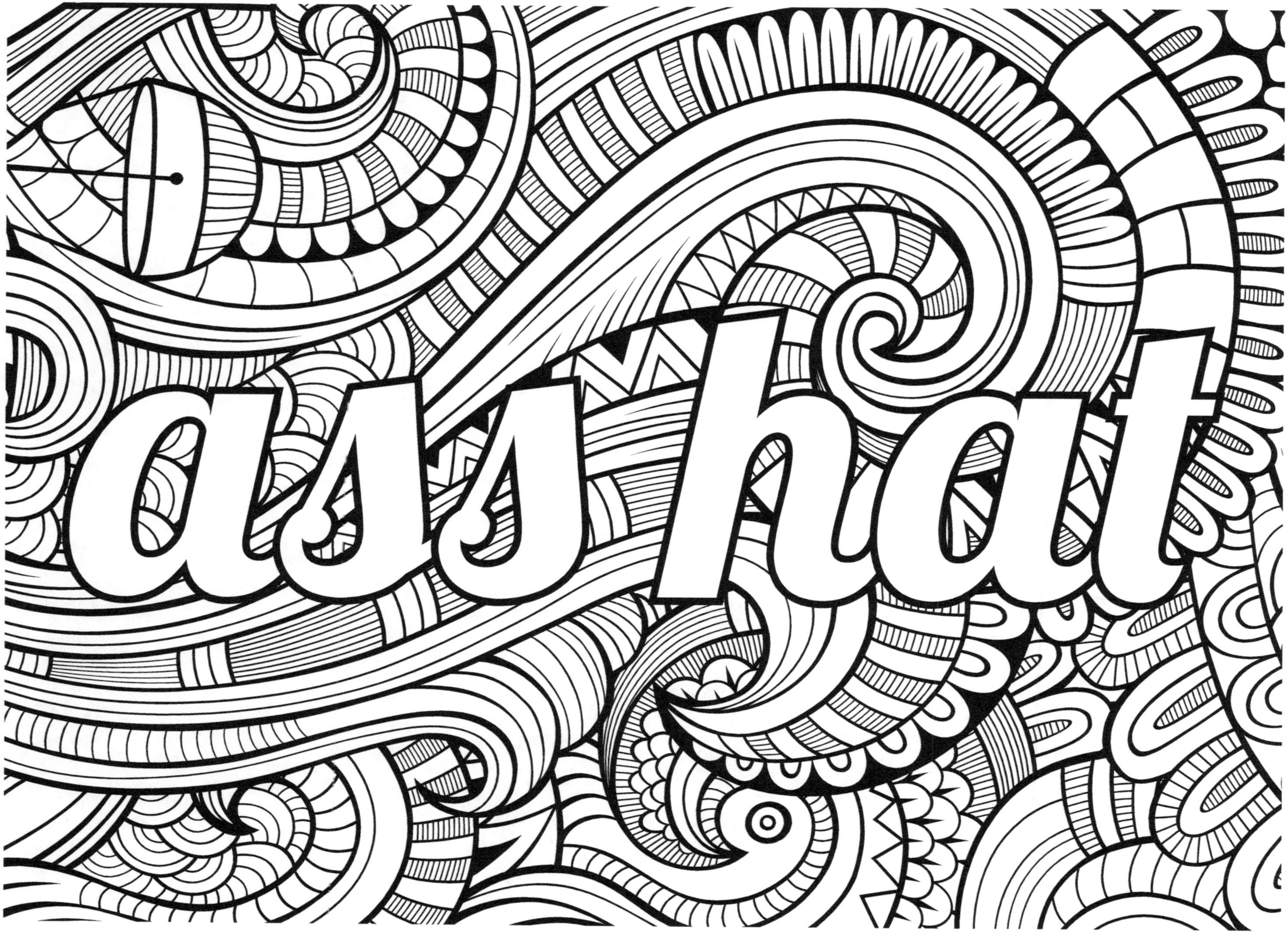
ass hat

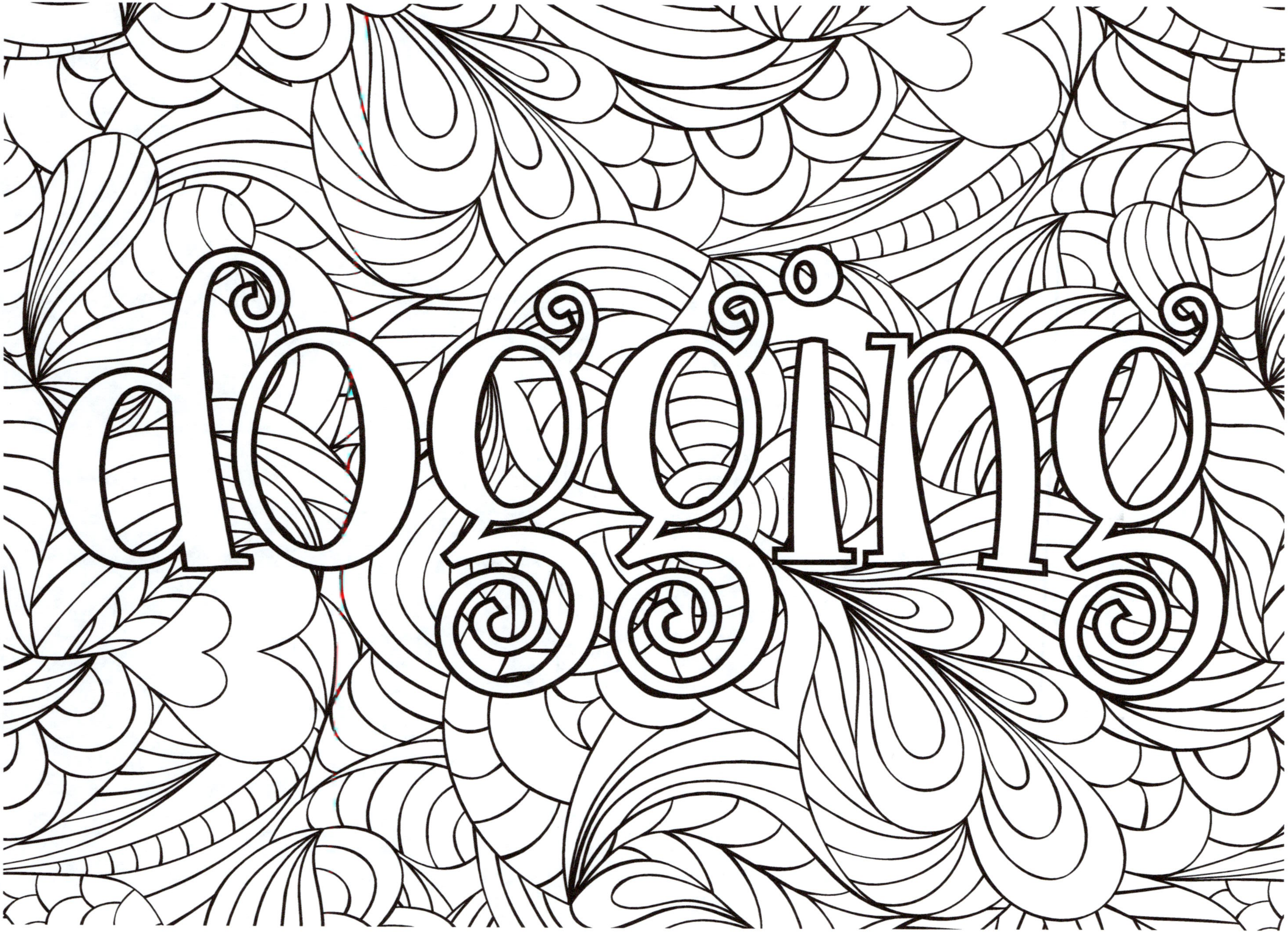
dogging

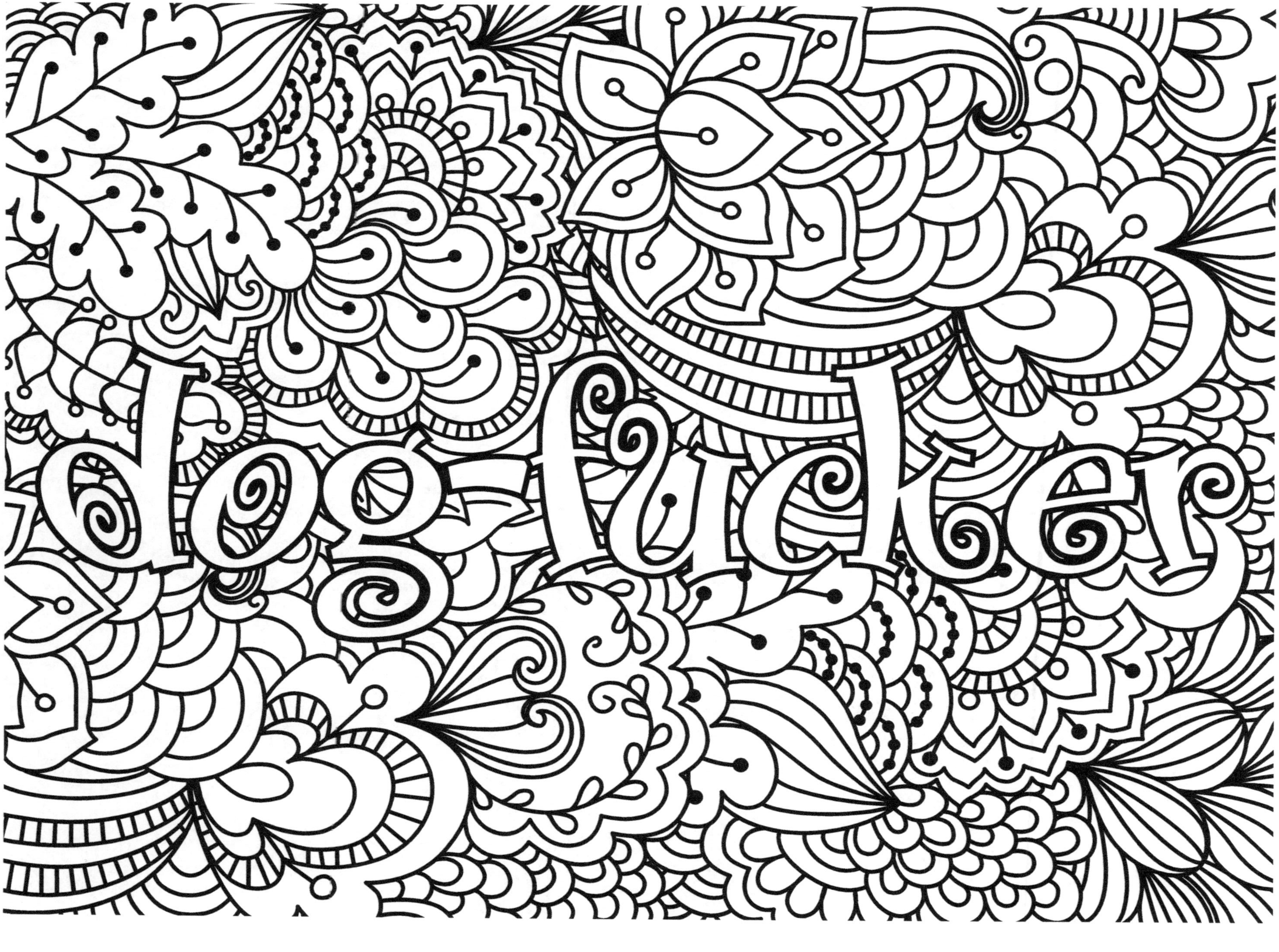
dog-fucker

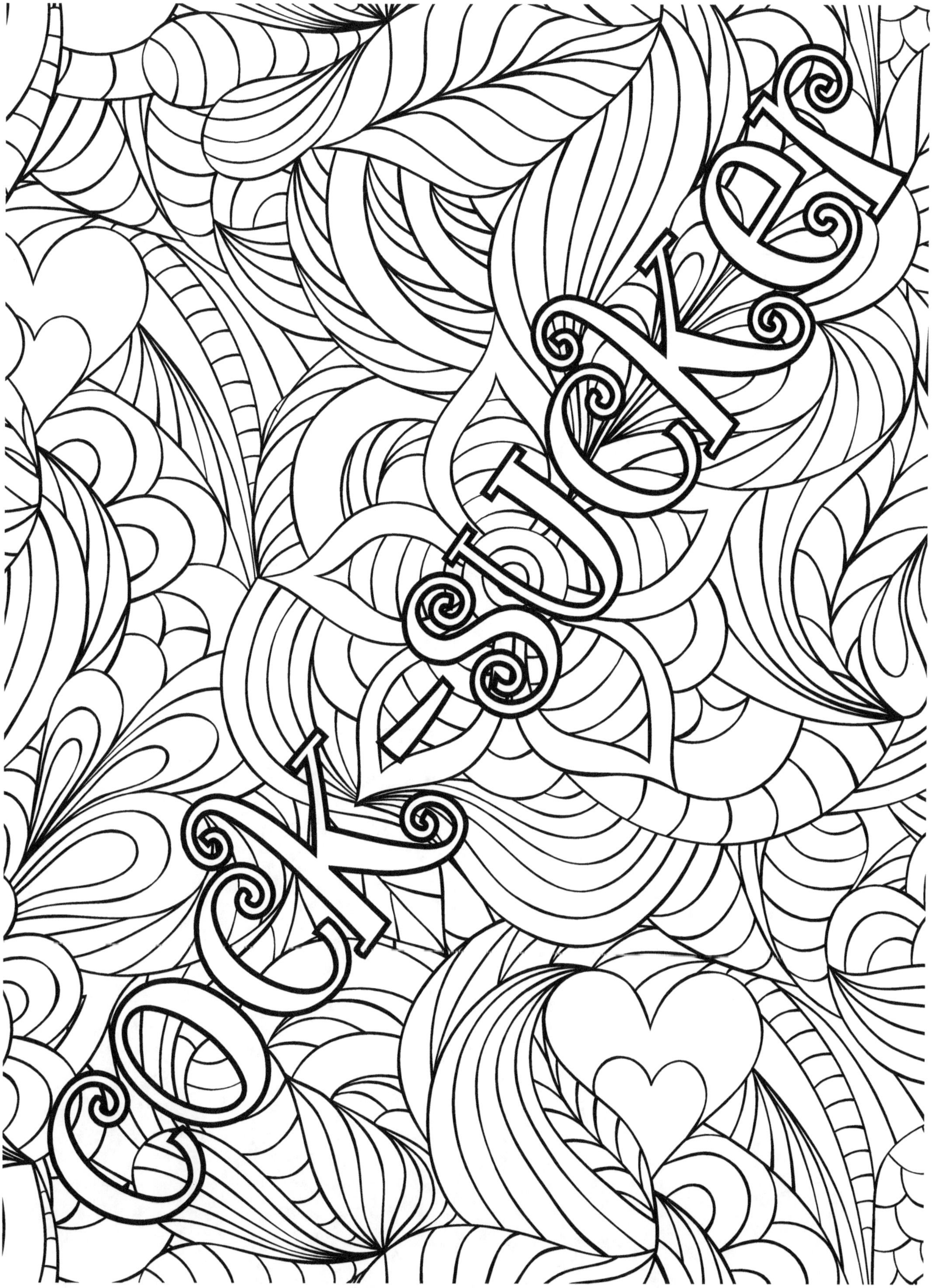
COCK-SUCKER

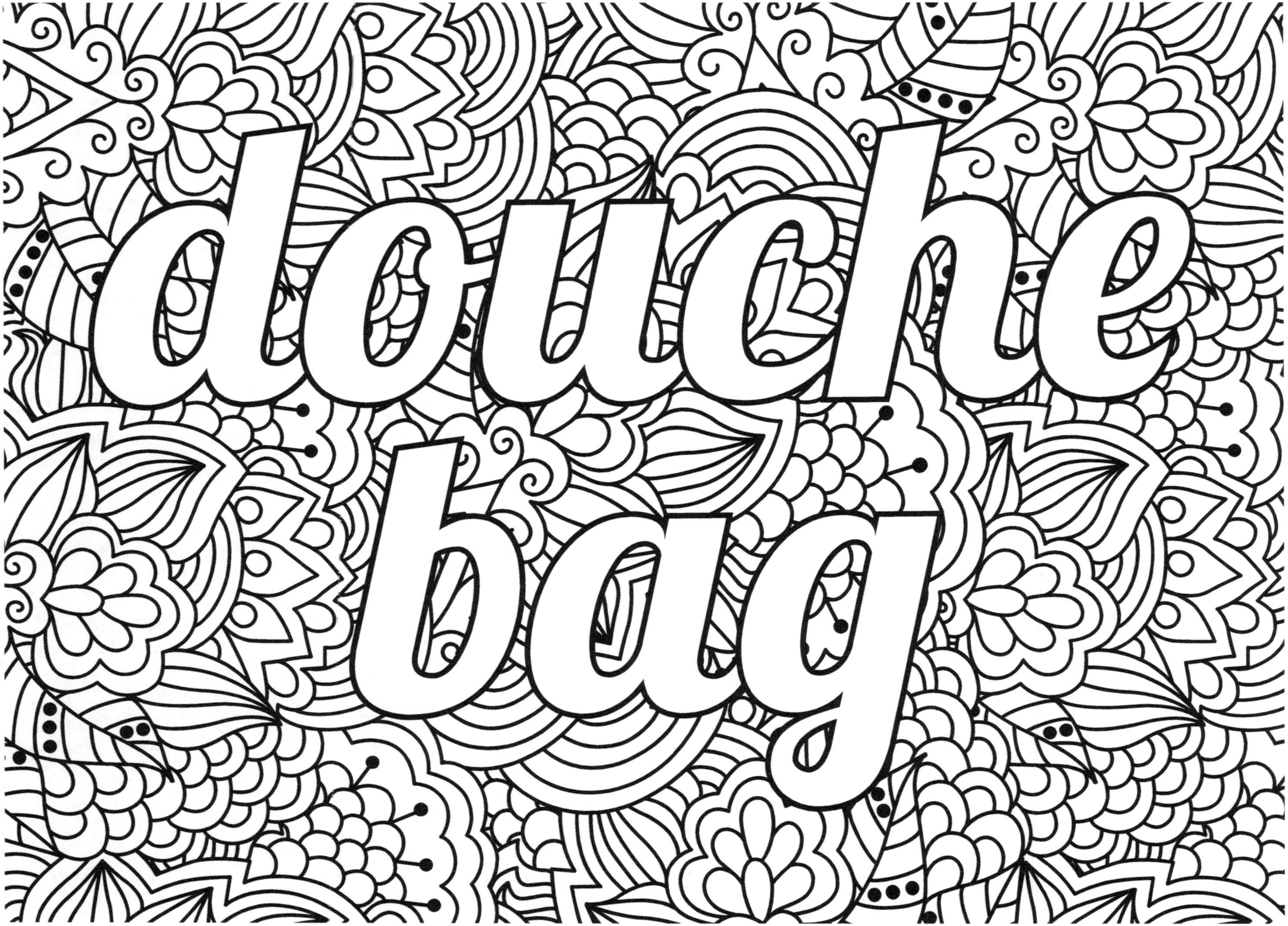
douche
bag

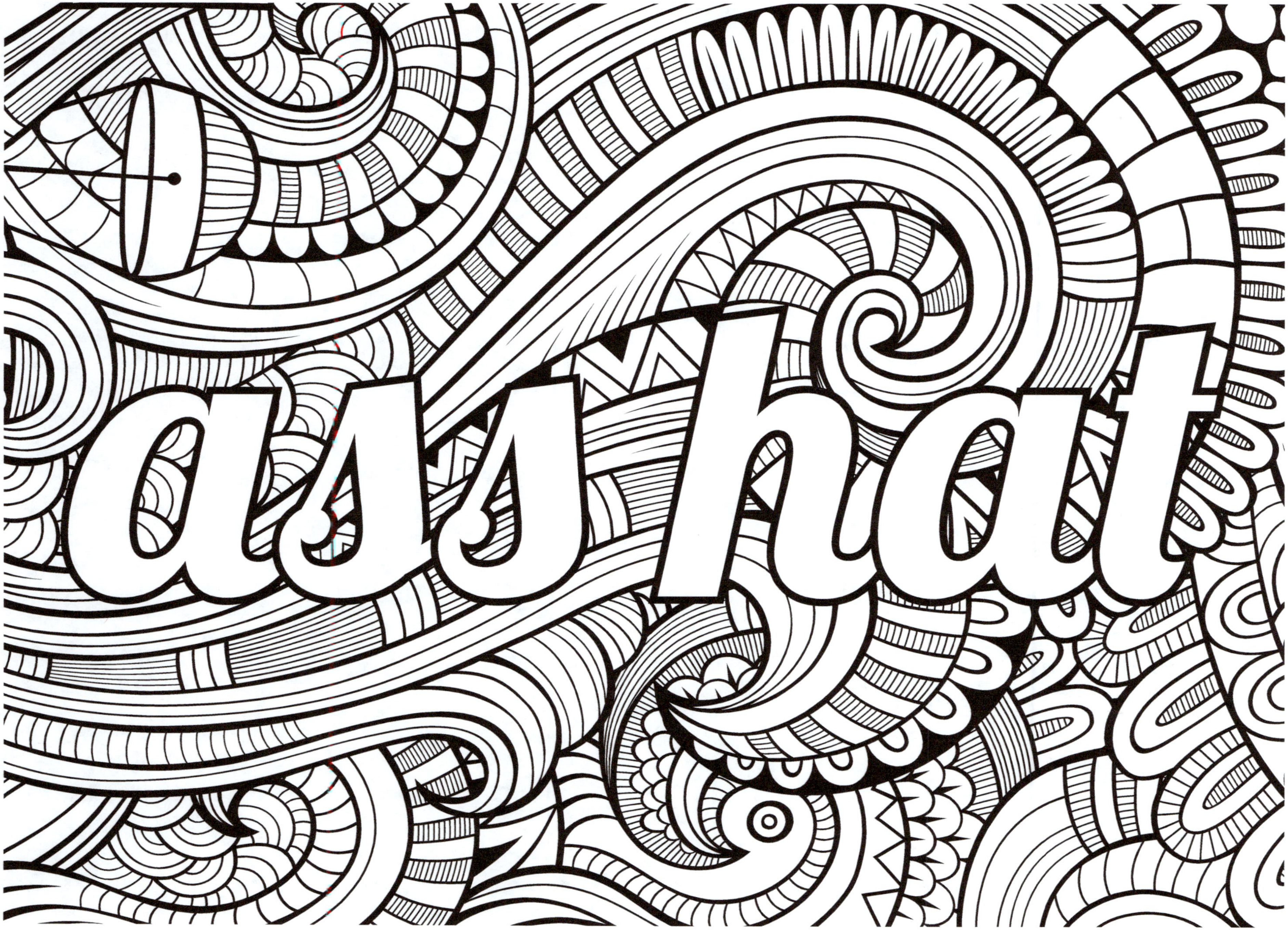
ass hat

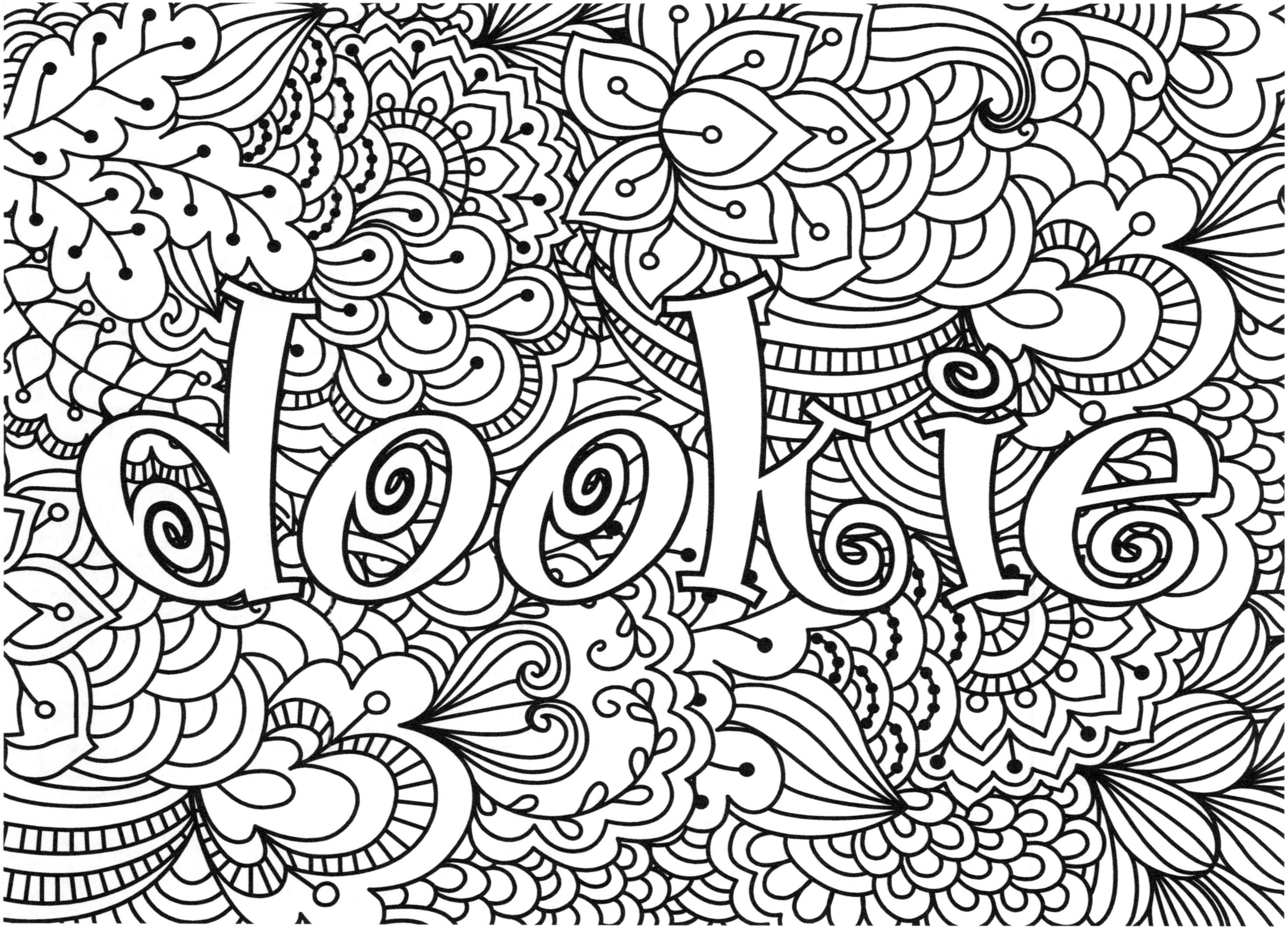
dookie

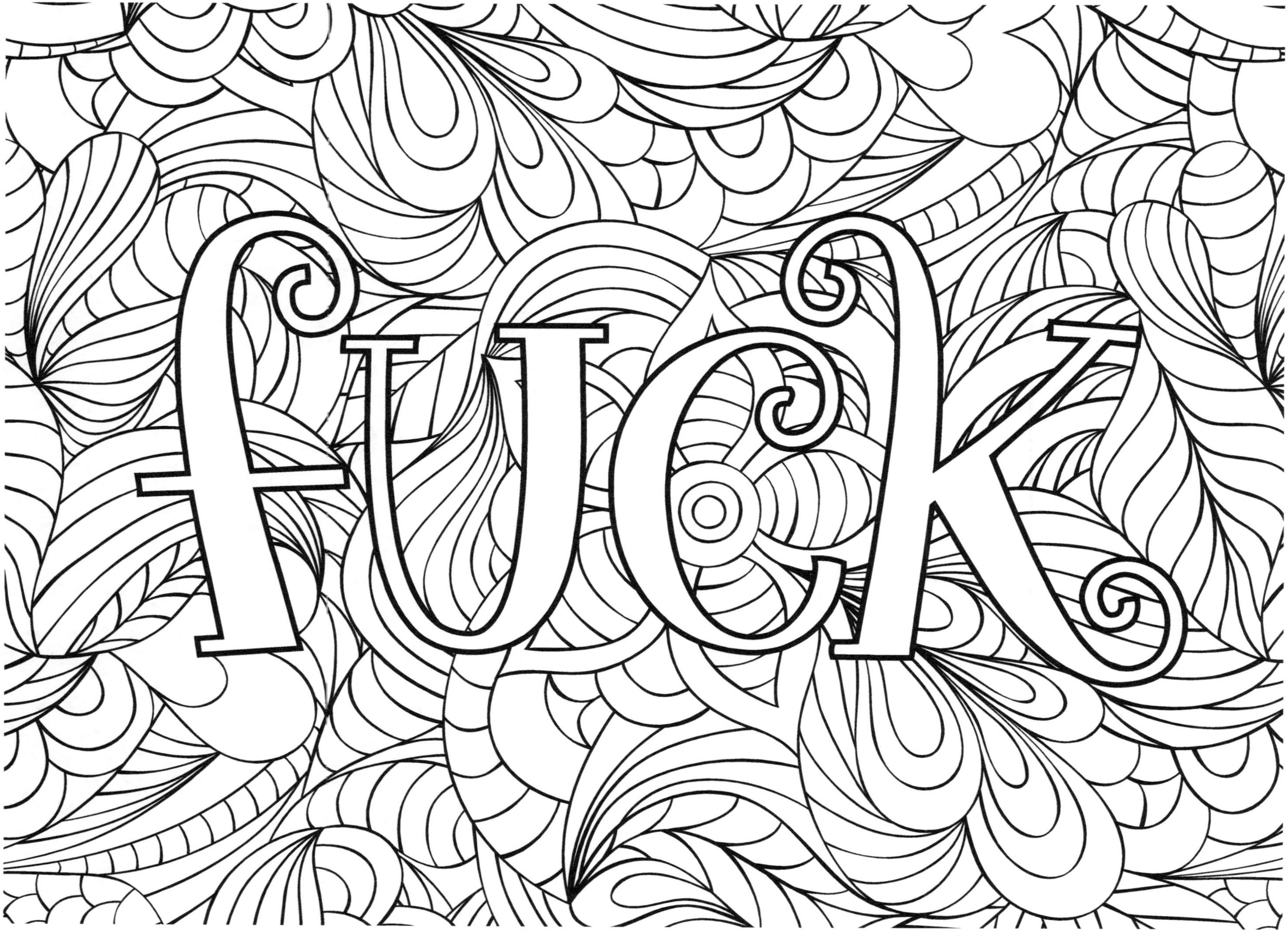
fuck

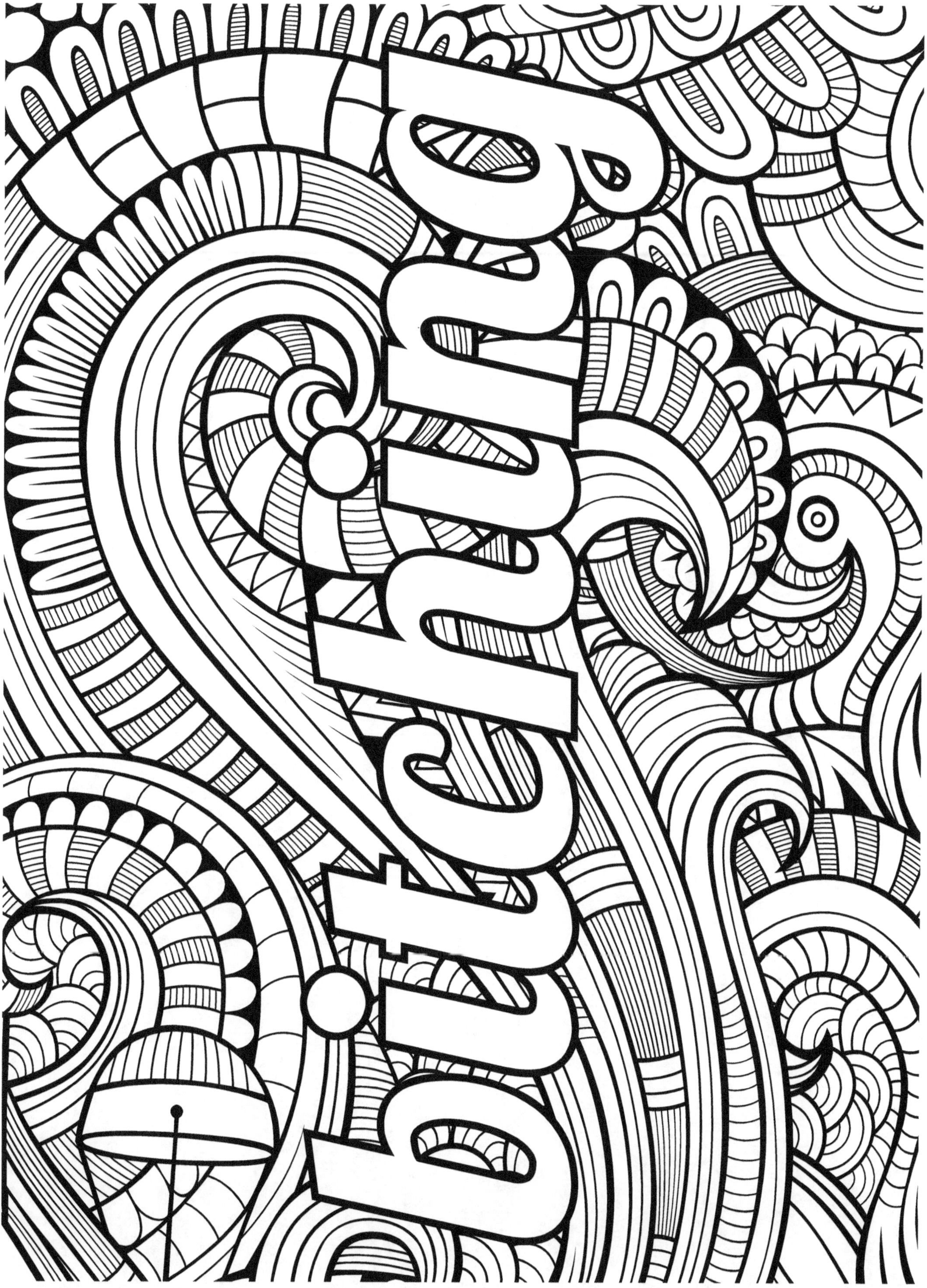
bitching

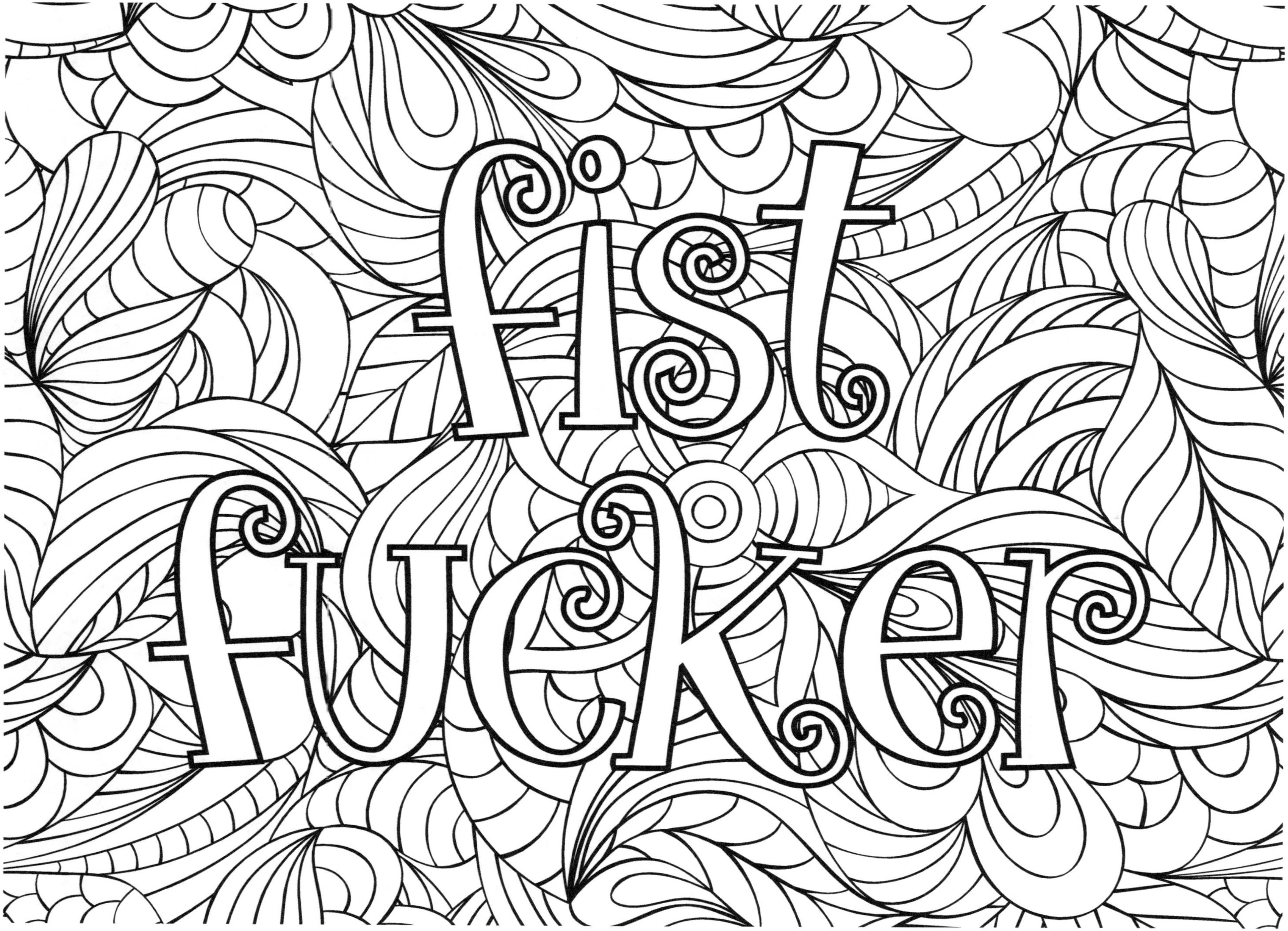
fist
fucker

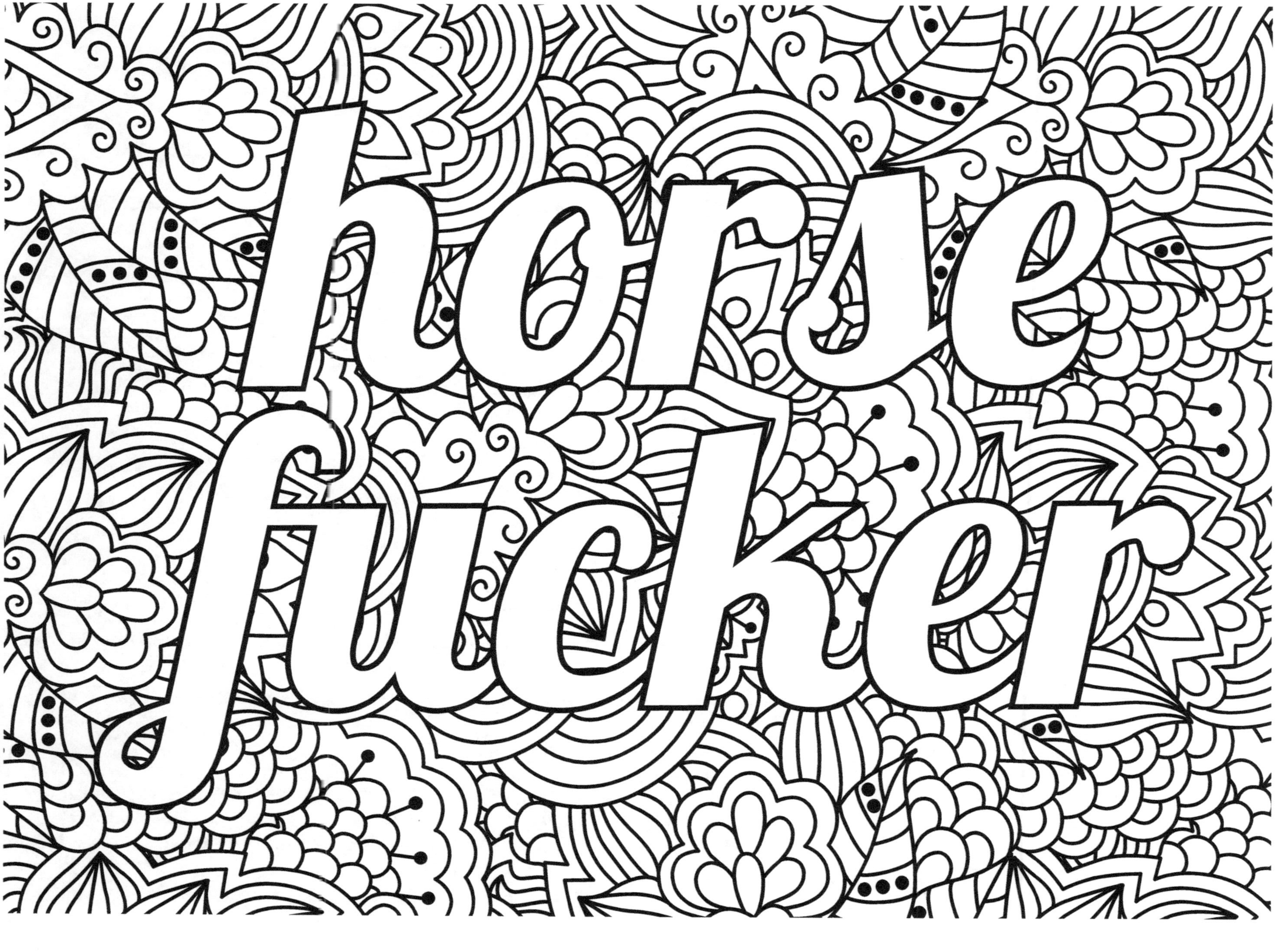
horse
fucker

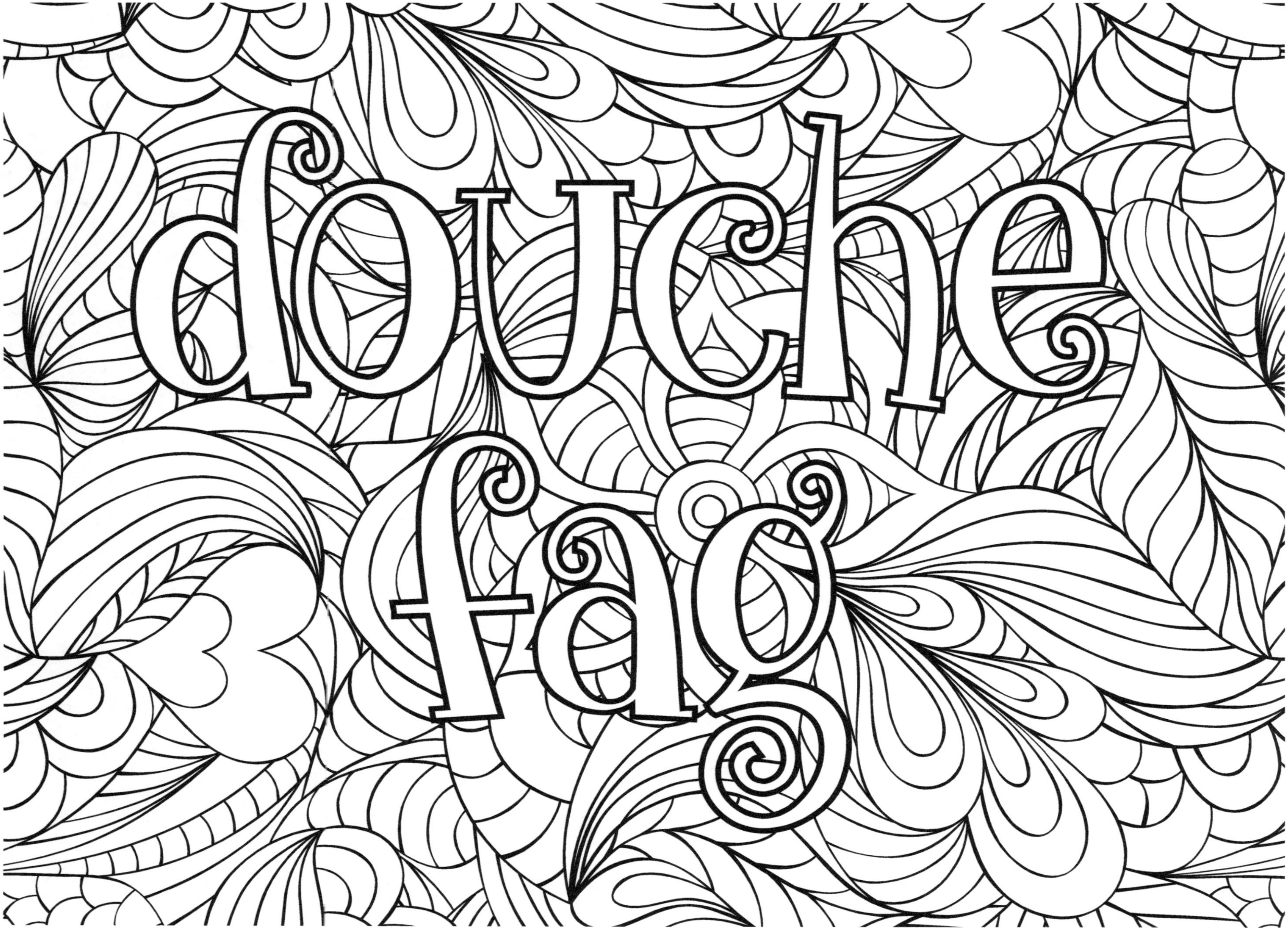
douche
fag

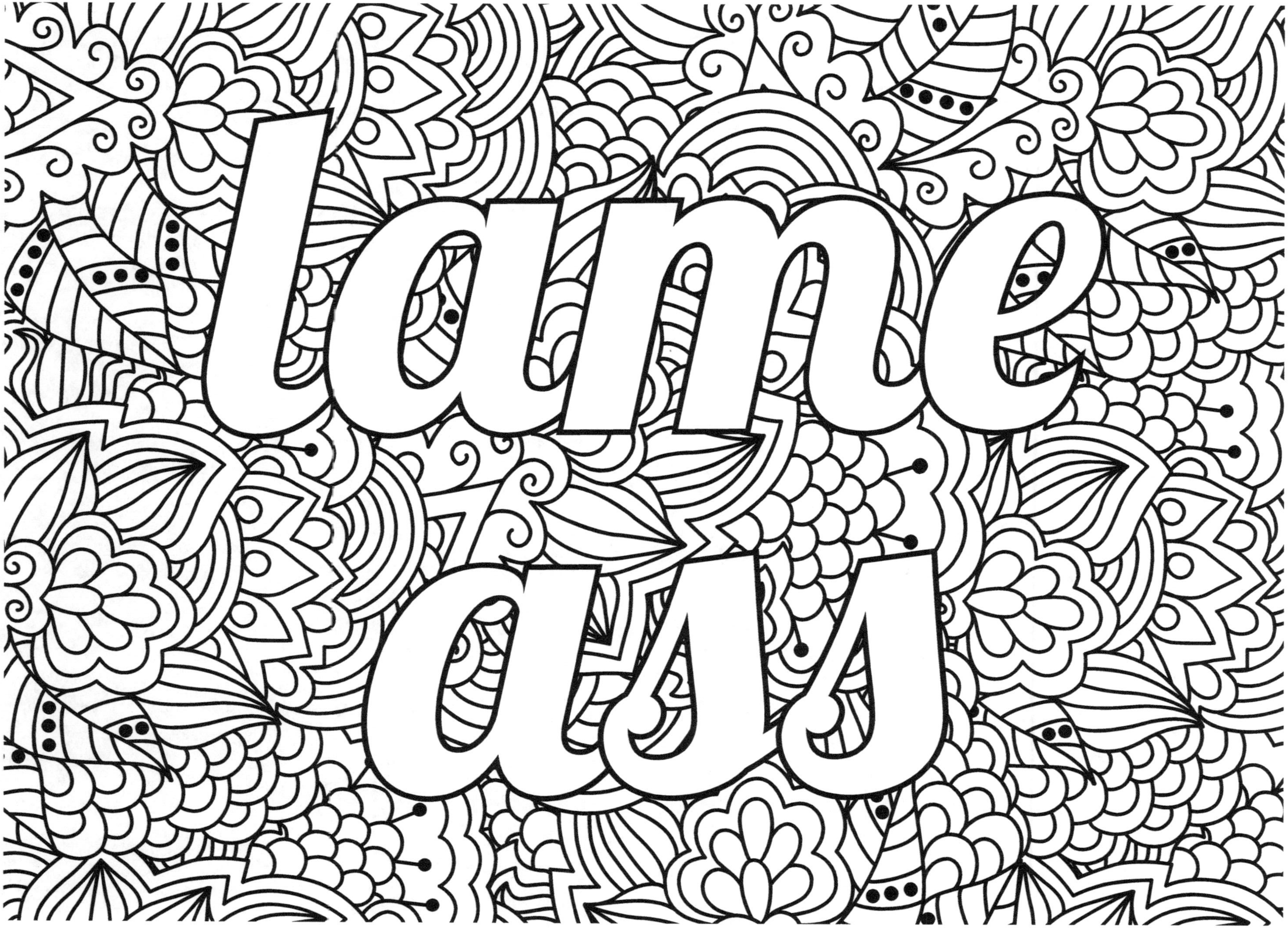
lame
ass

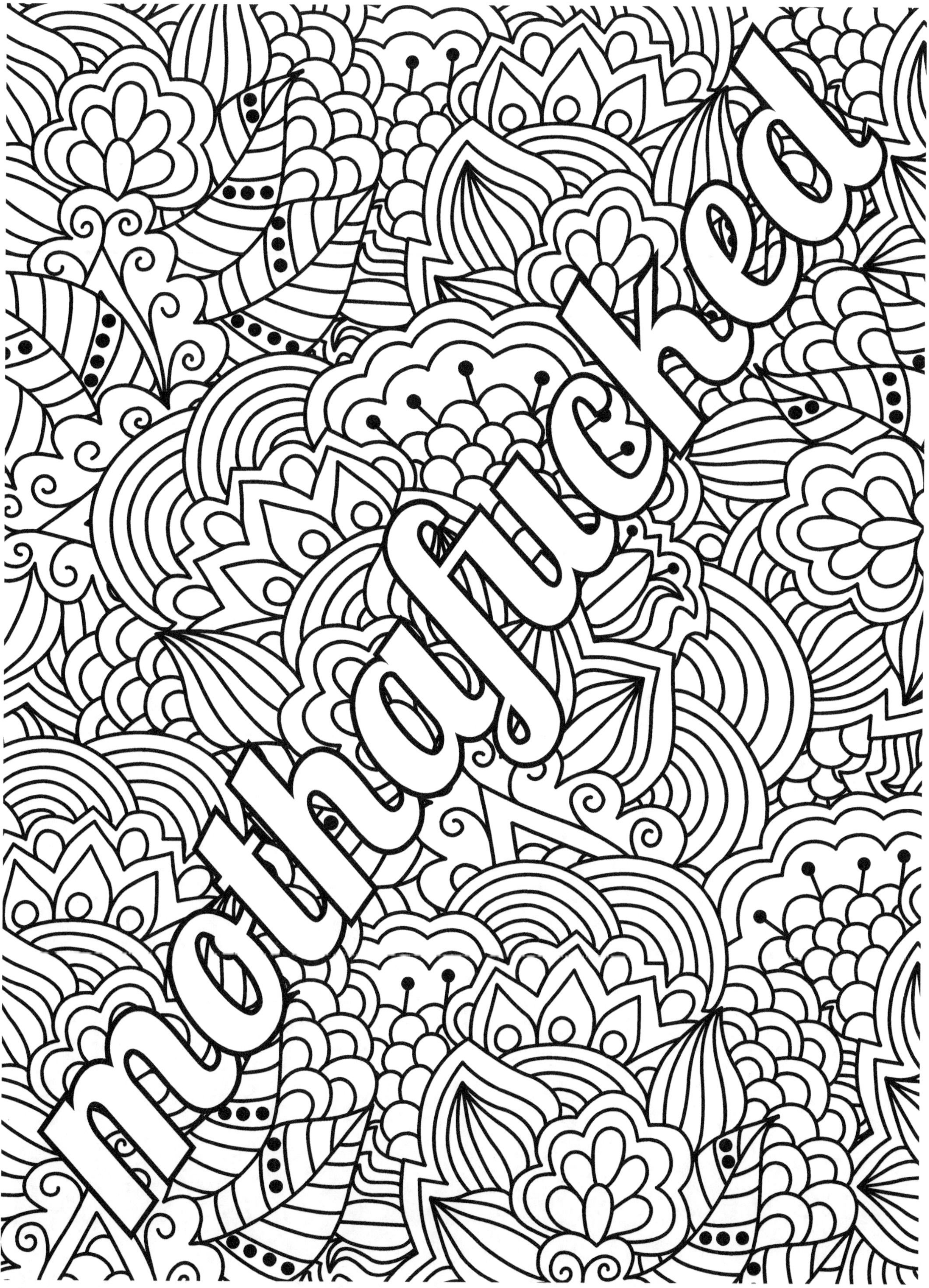
mothafucked

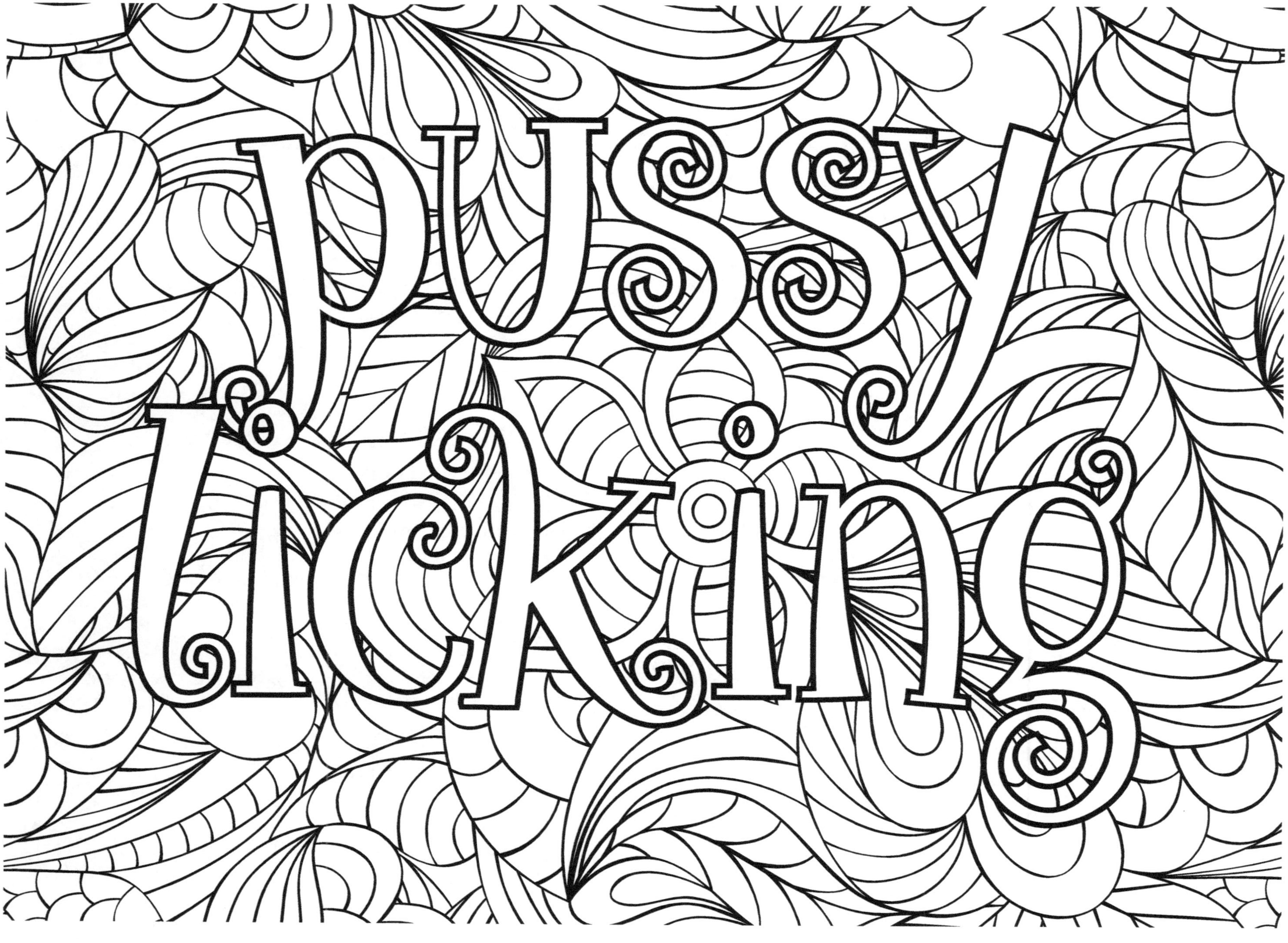
pussy
licking

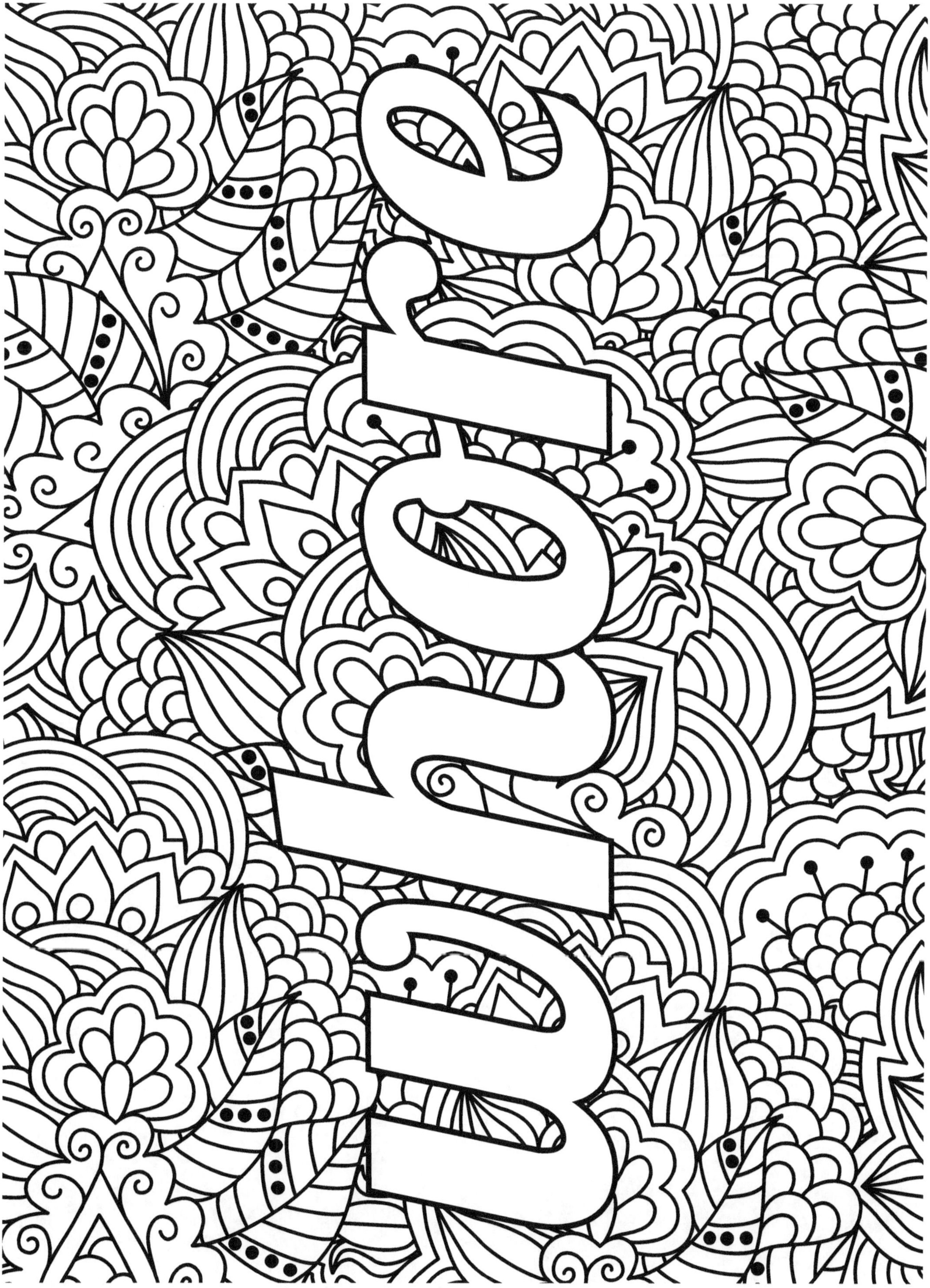
more

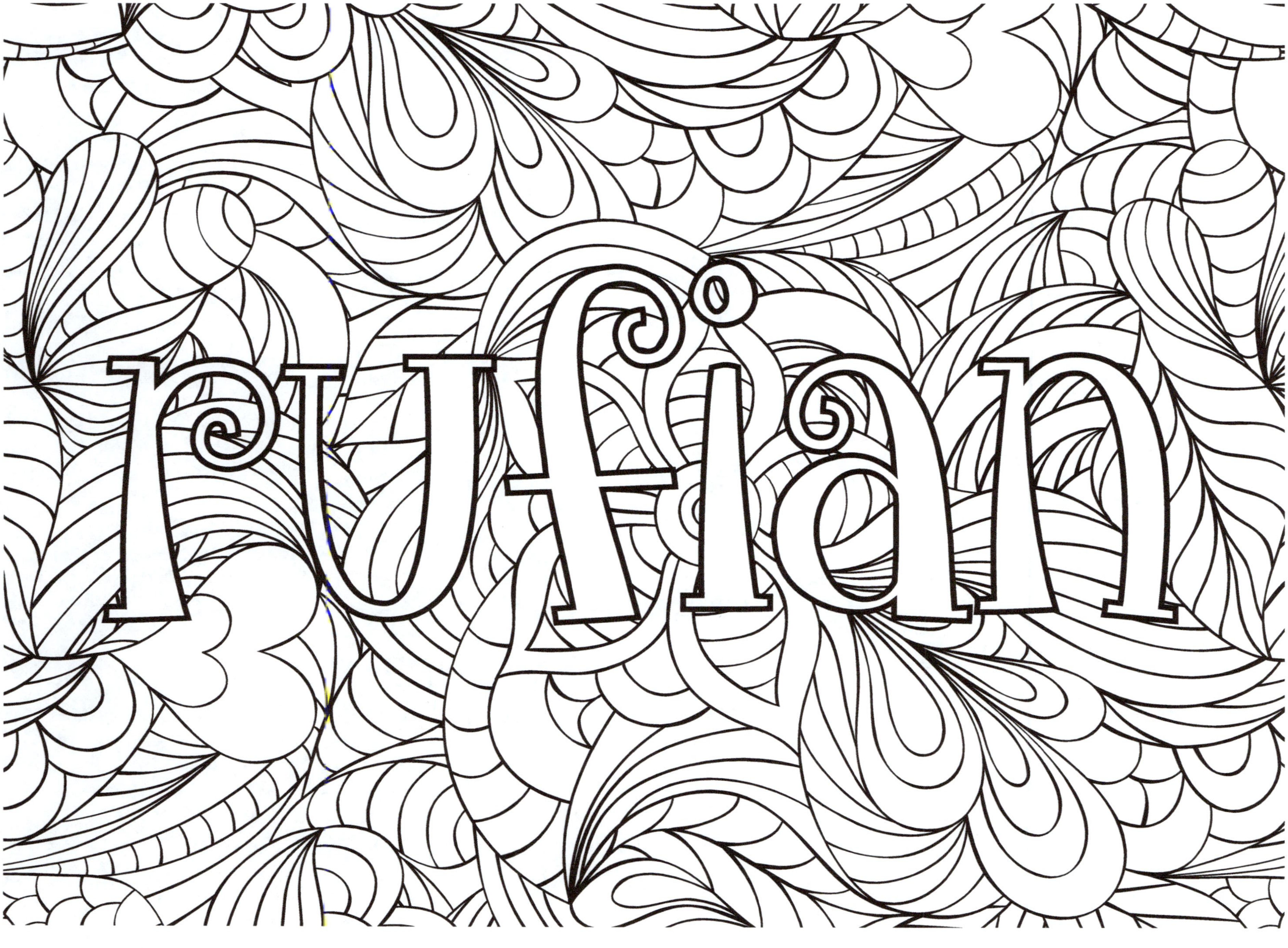
ruffian

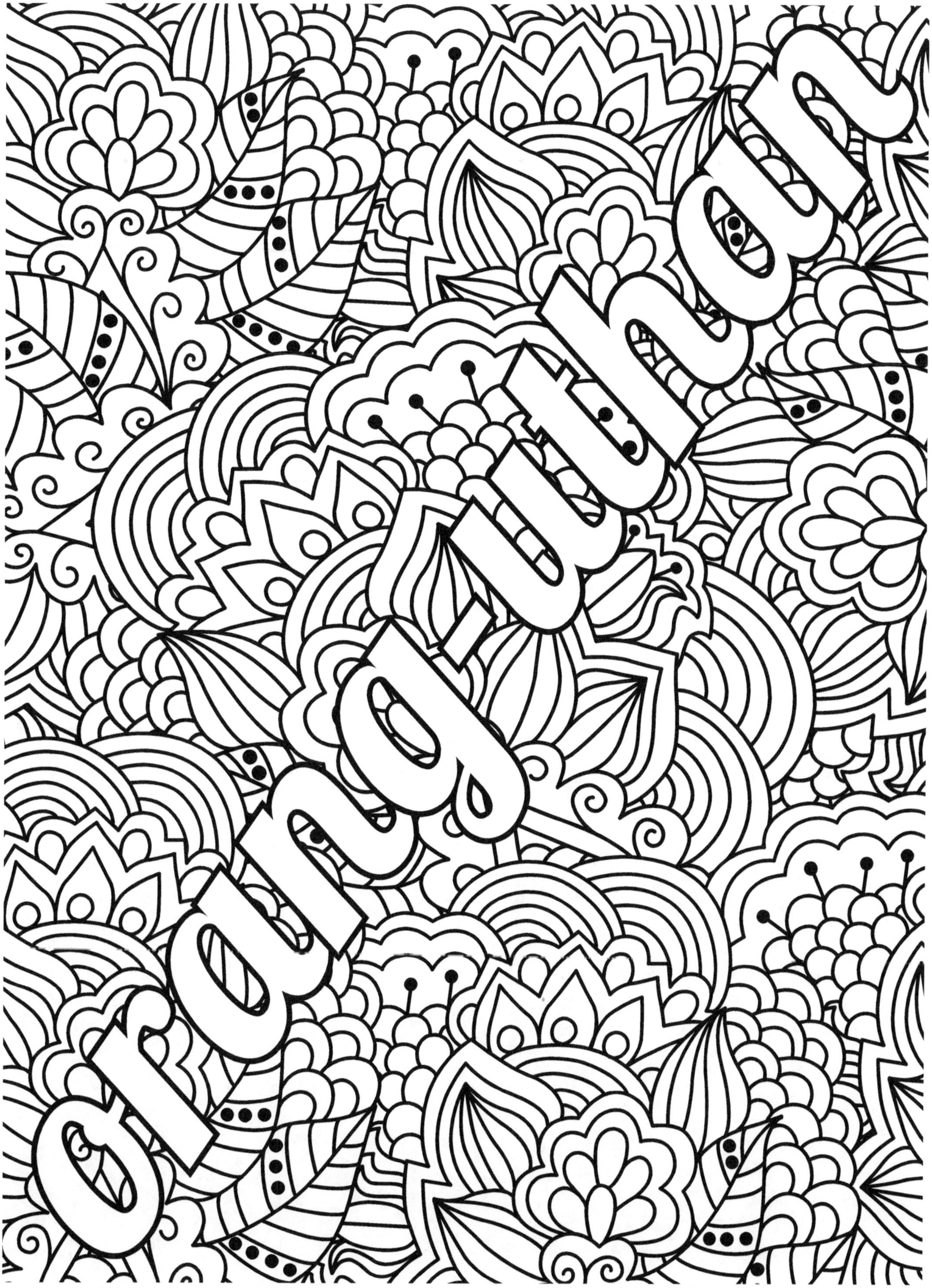
orang-uthan

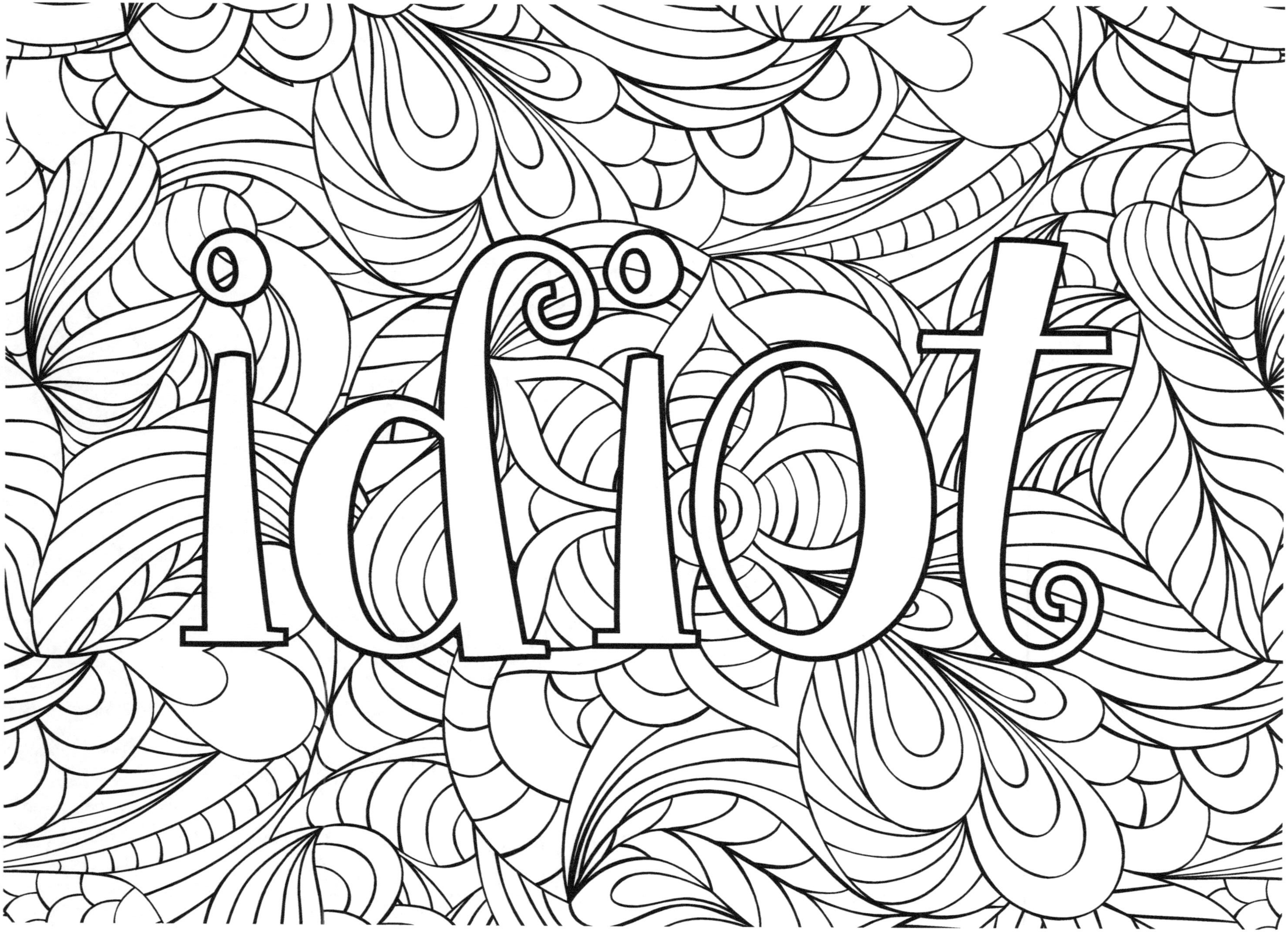
idiot

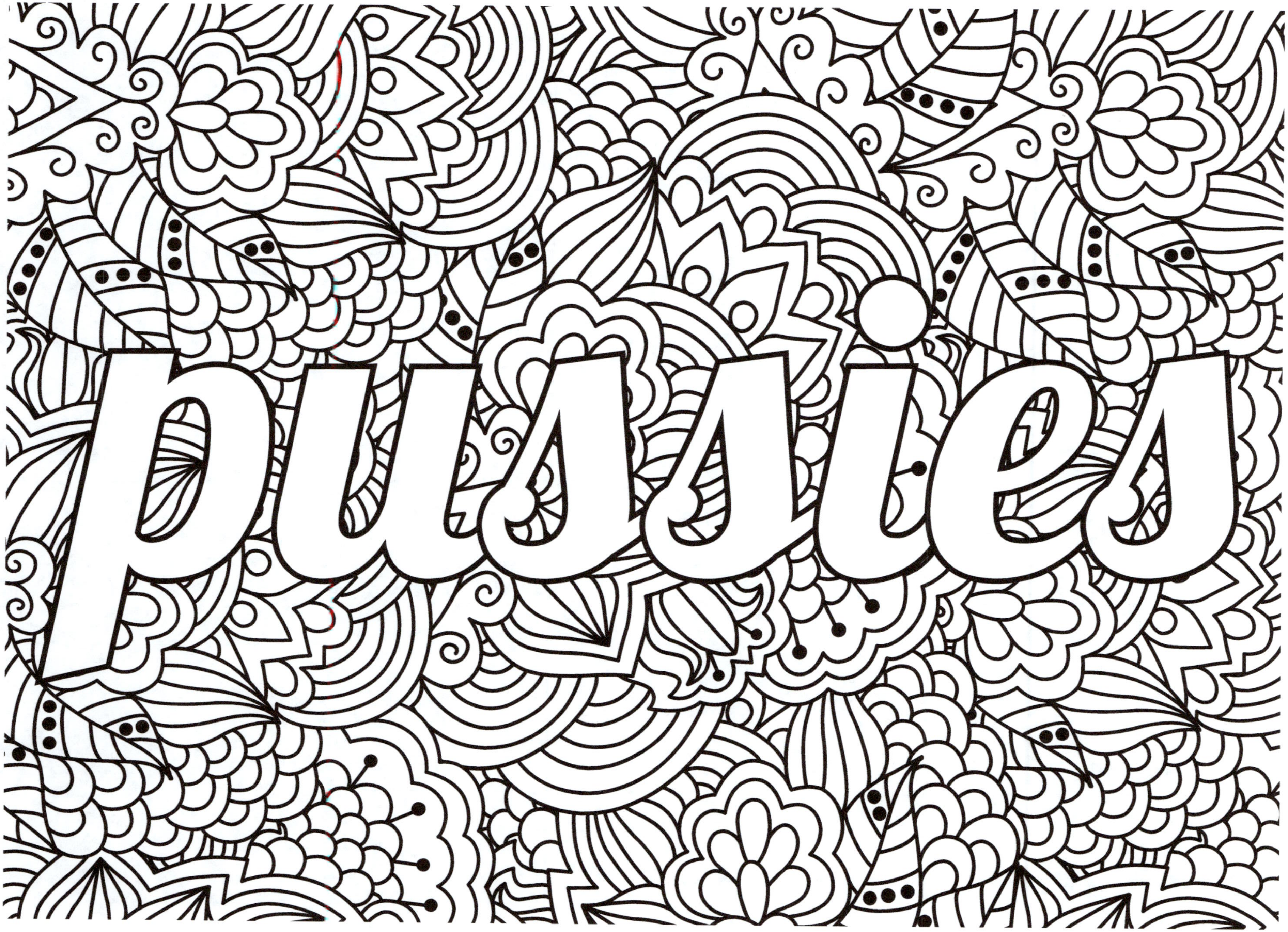
pussies

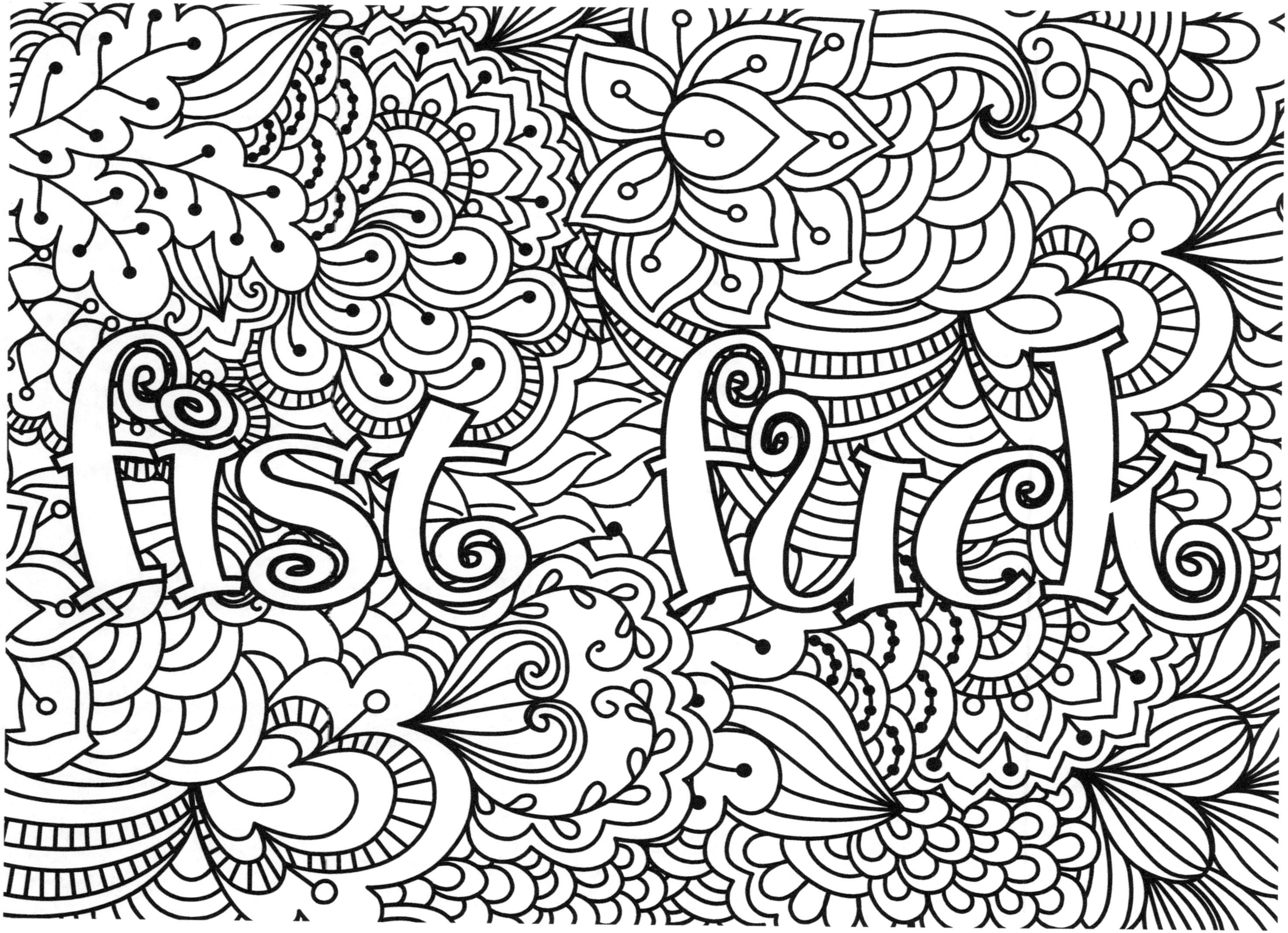
fist fuck

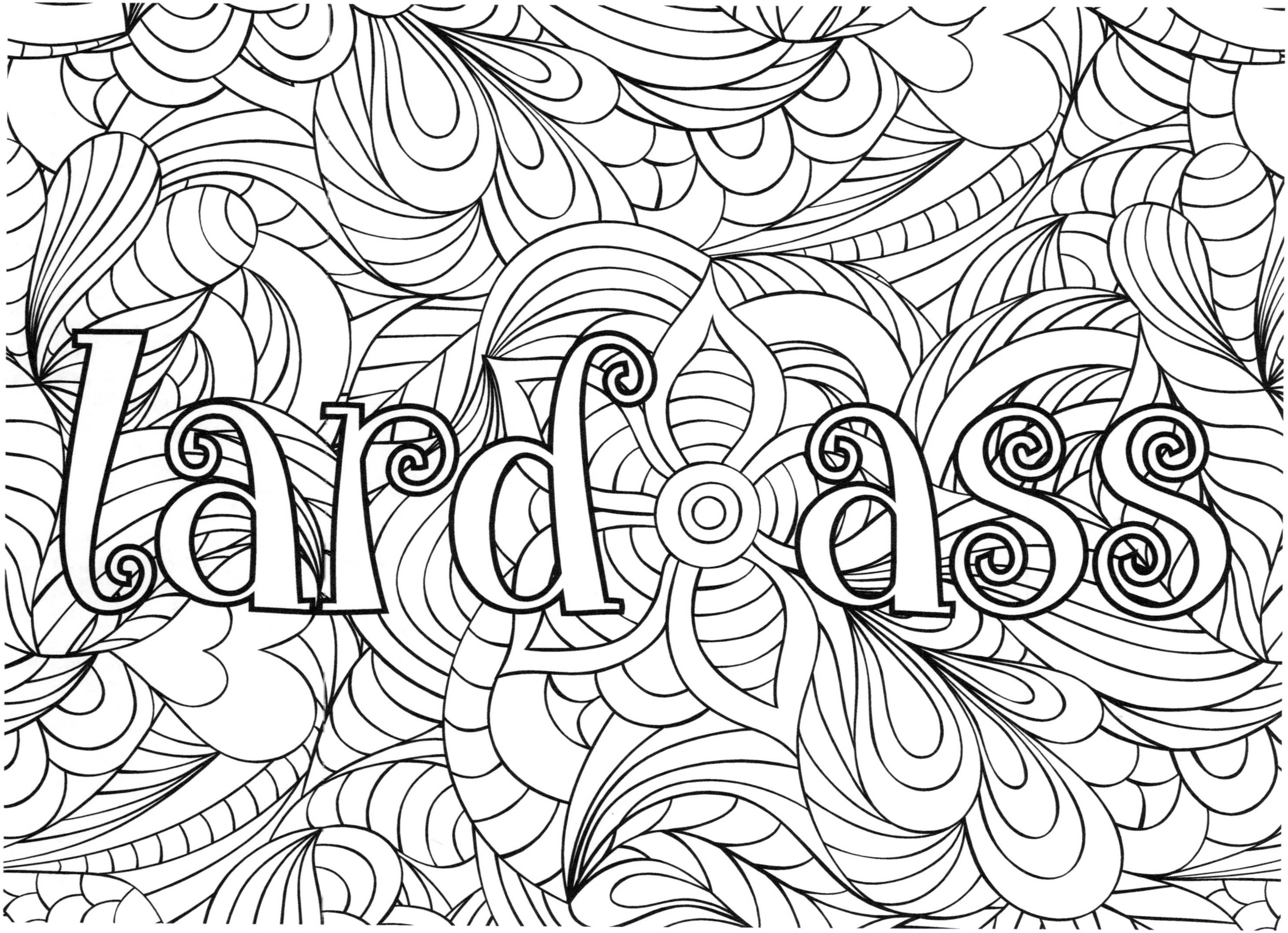
lardass

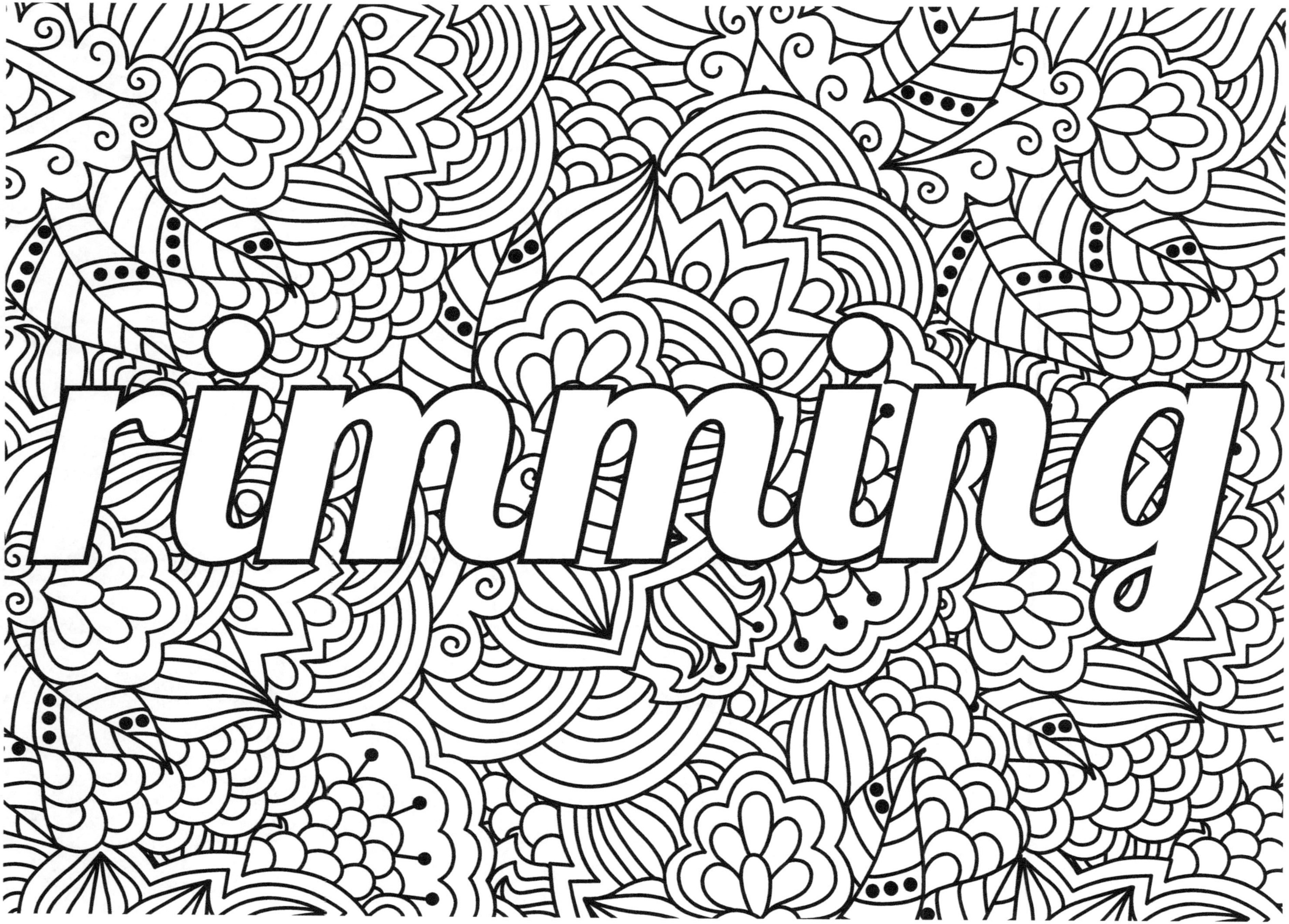
rimming

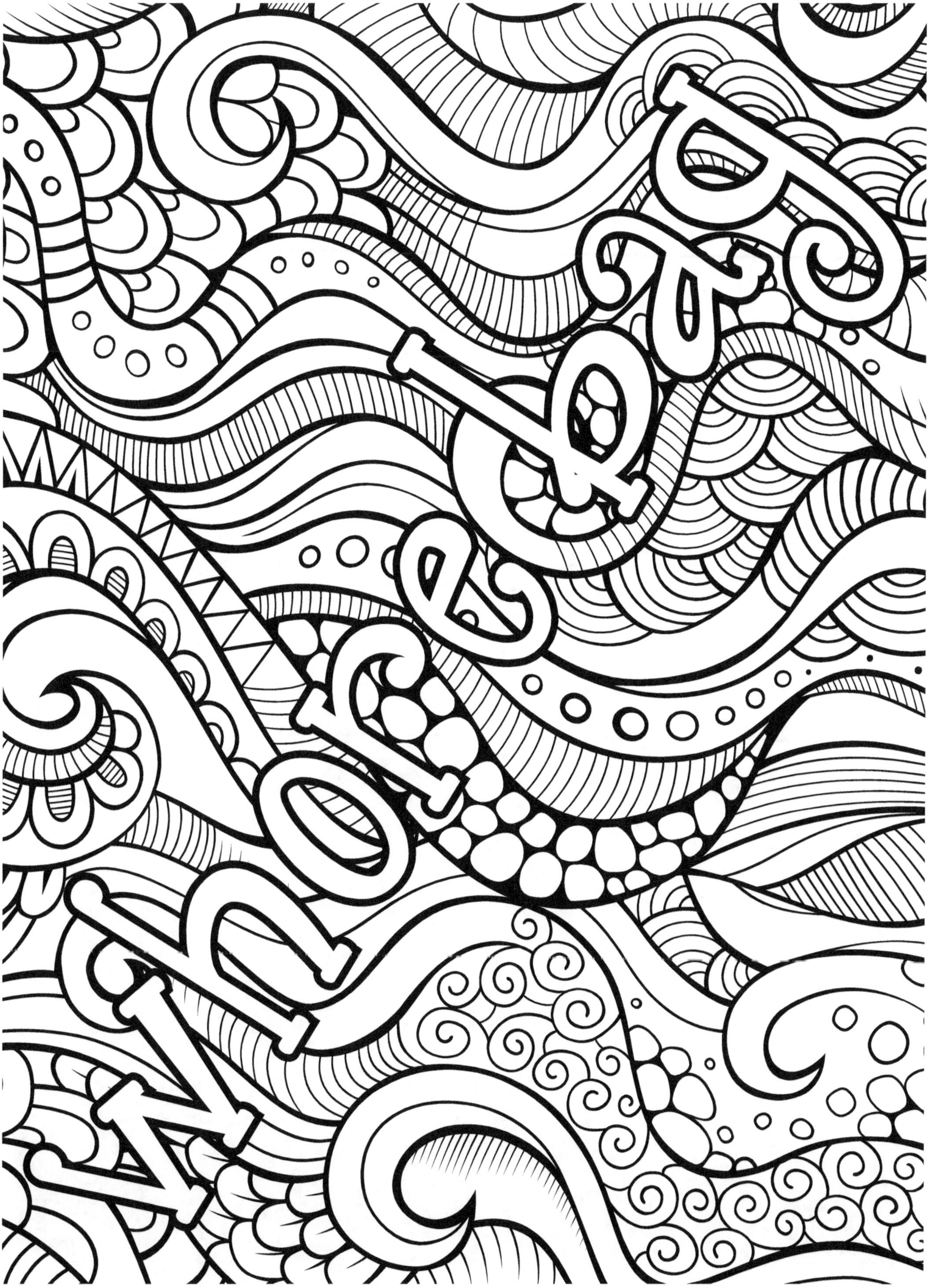

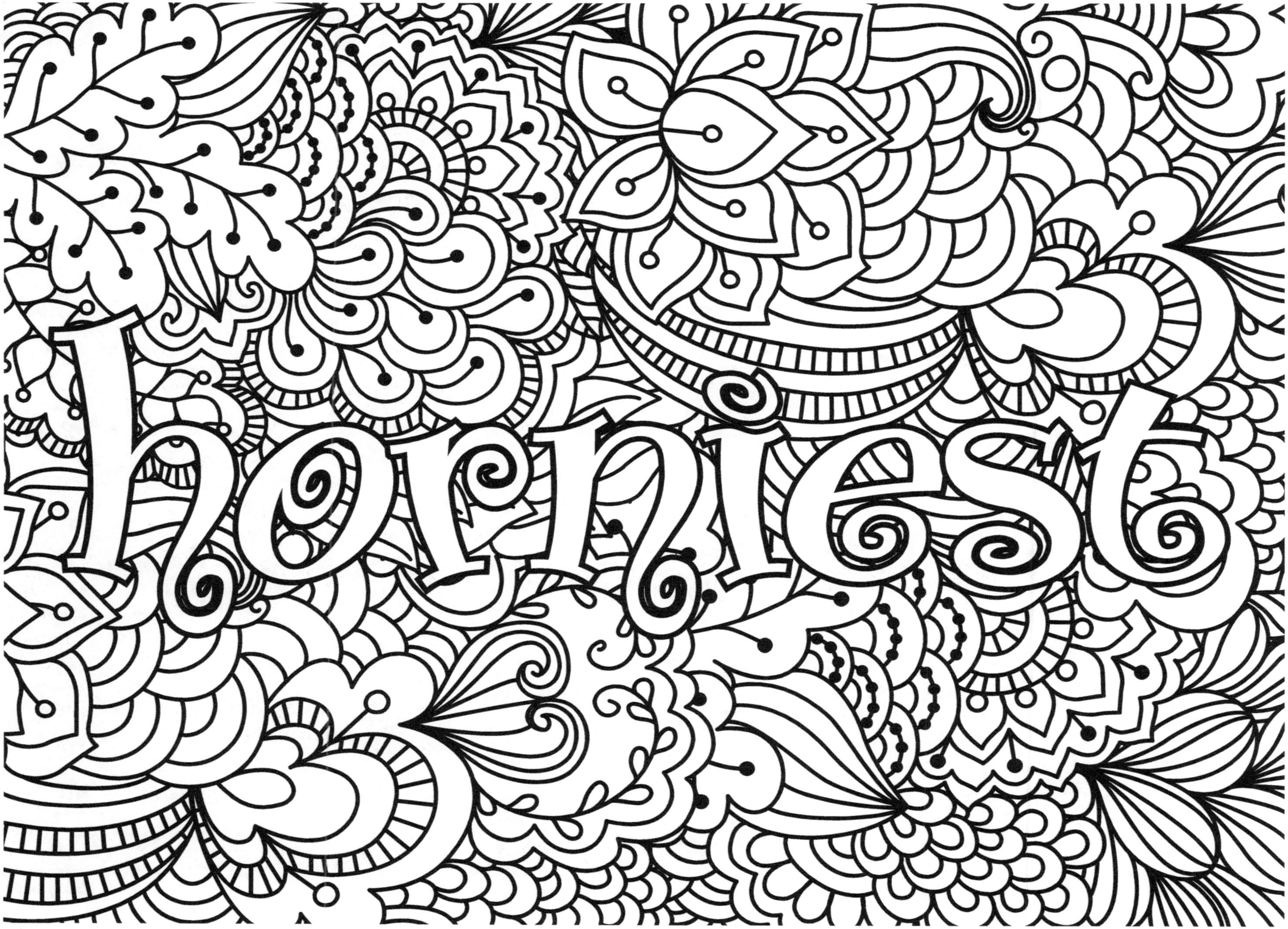
horniest

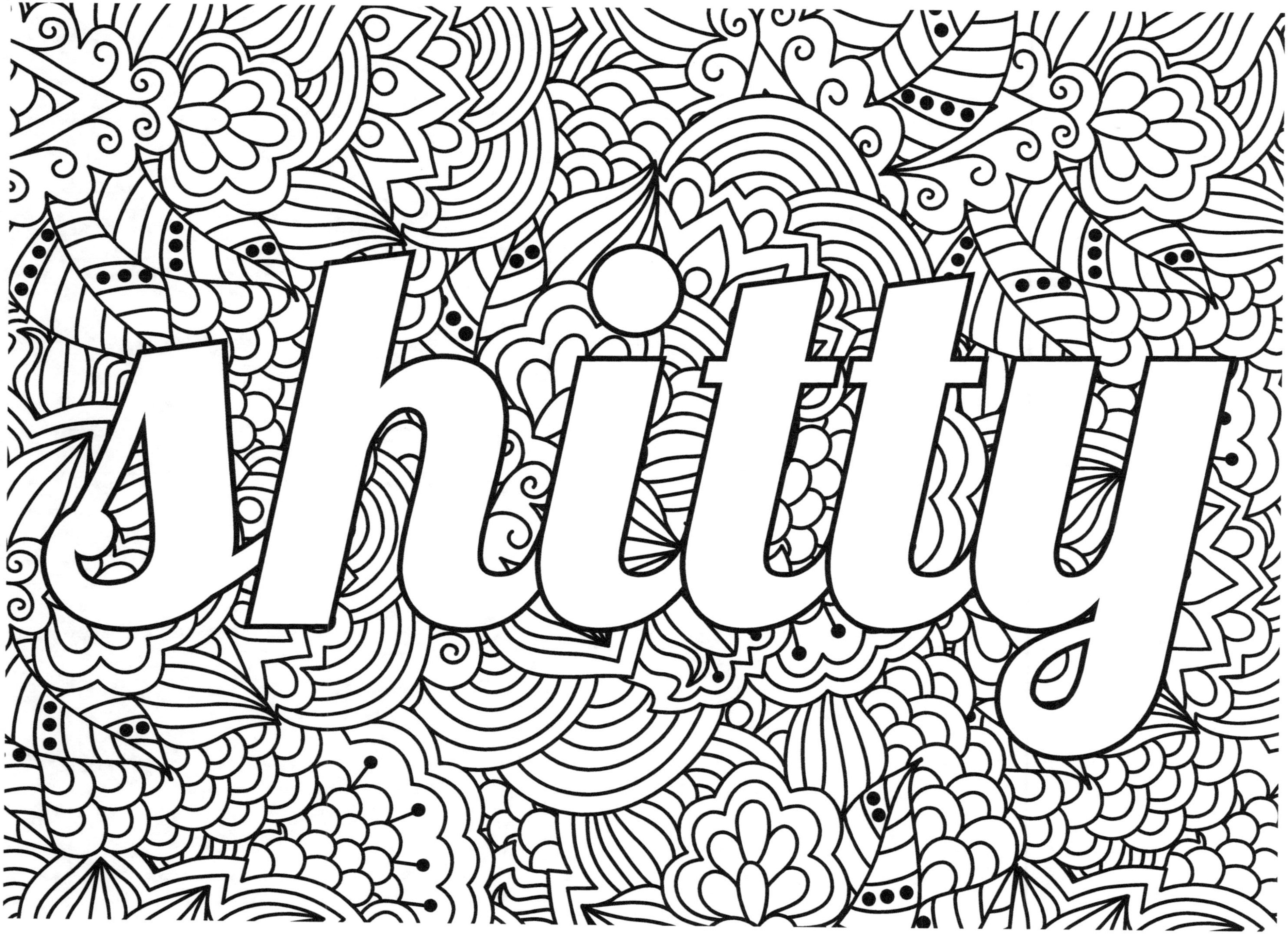
shitty

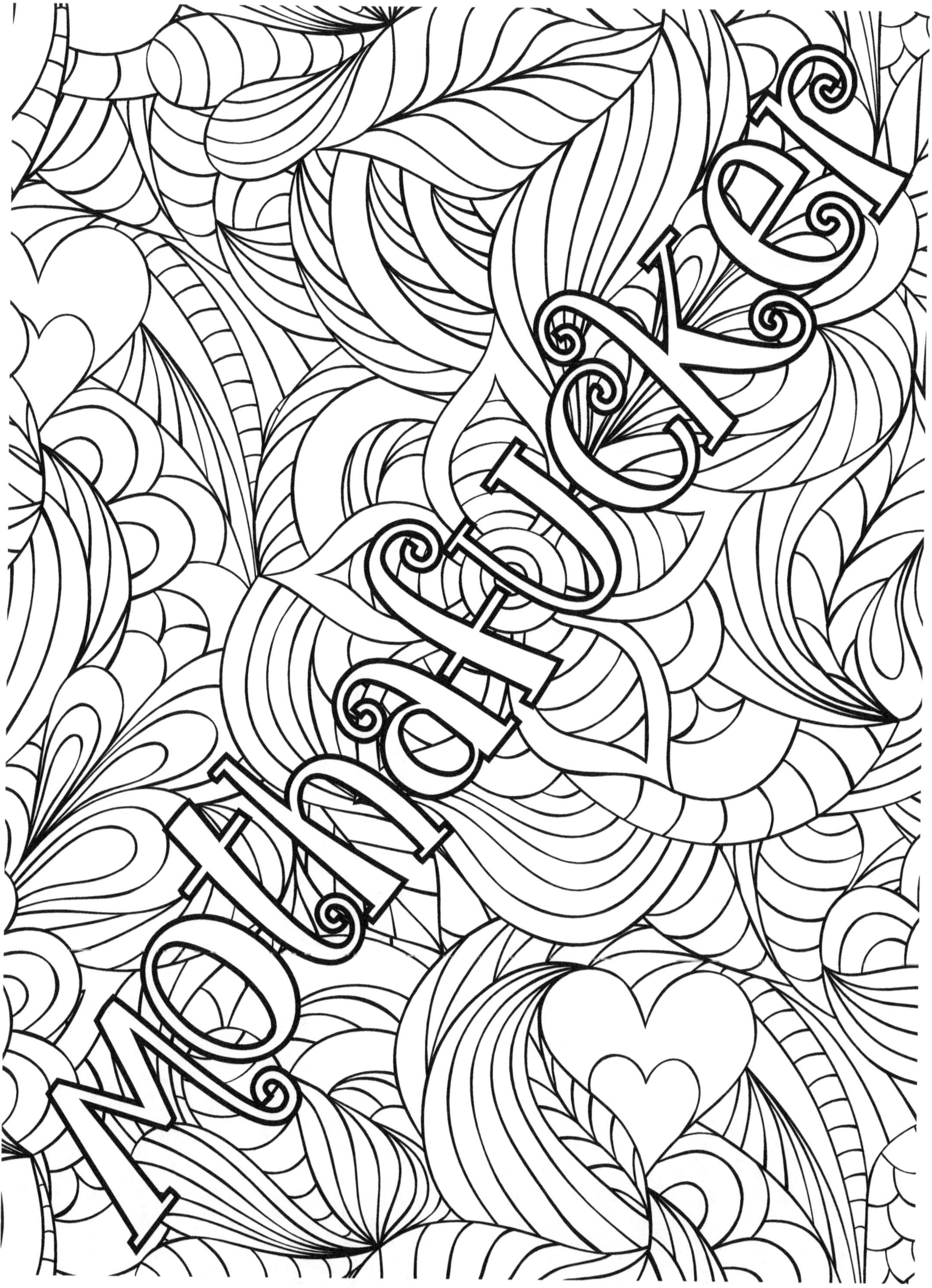
Motherfucker

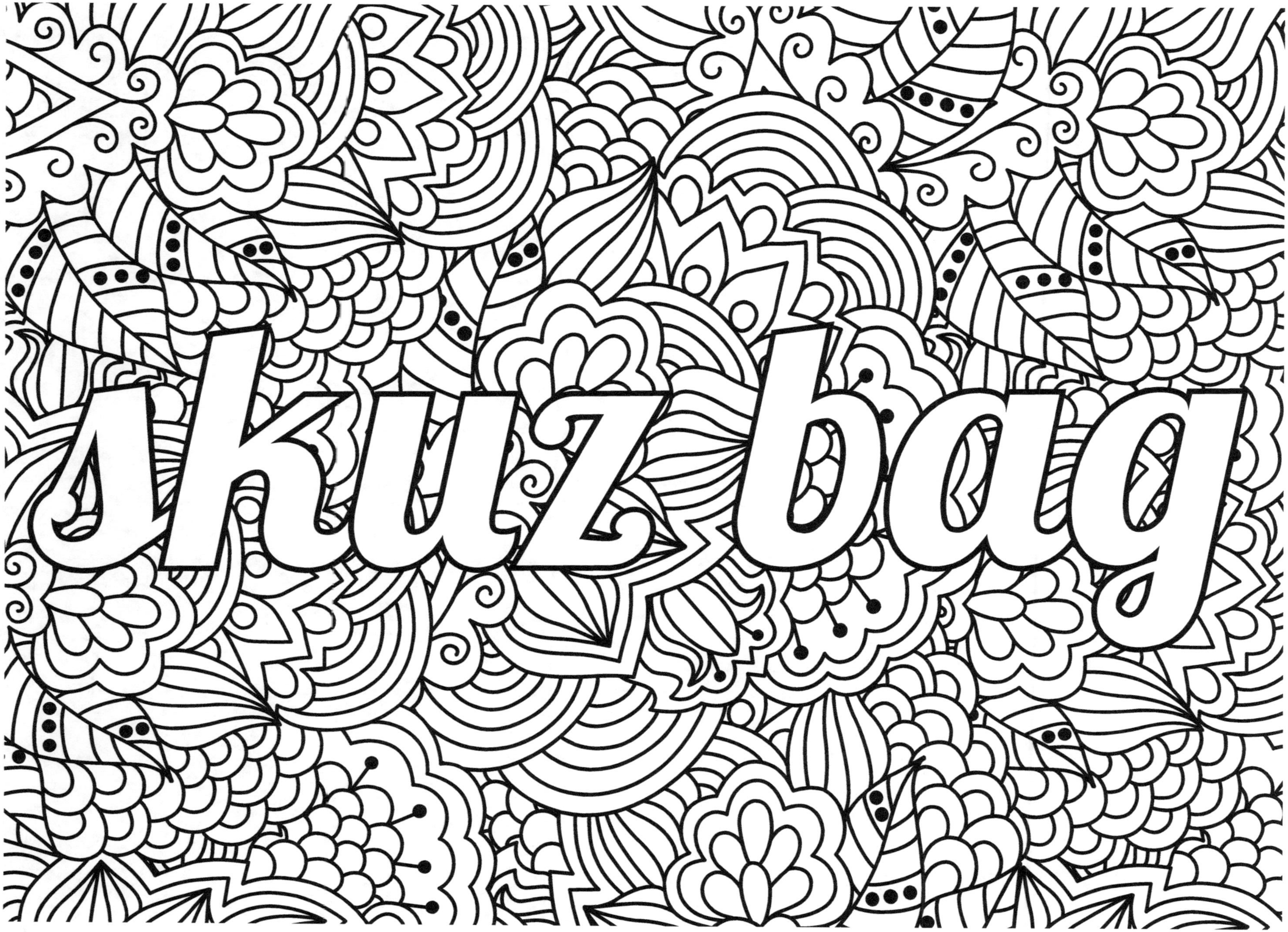
skuz bag

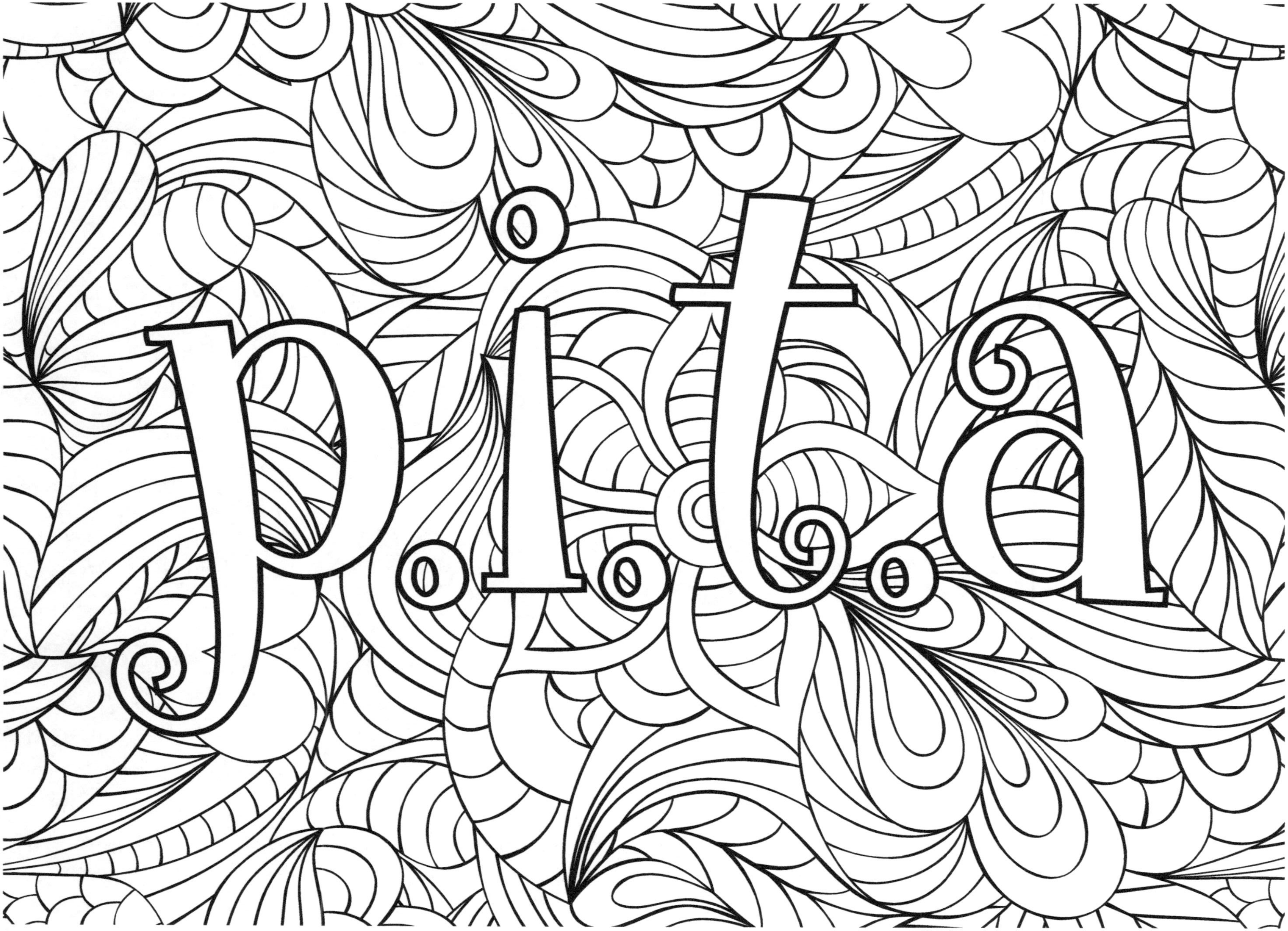
p.i.t.a

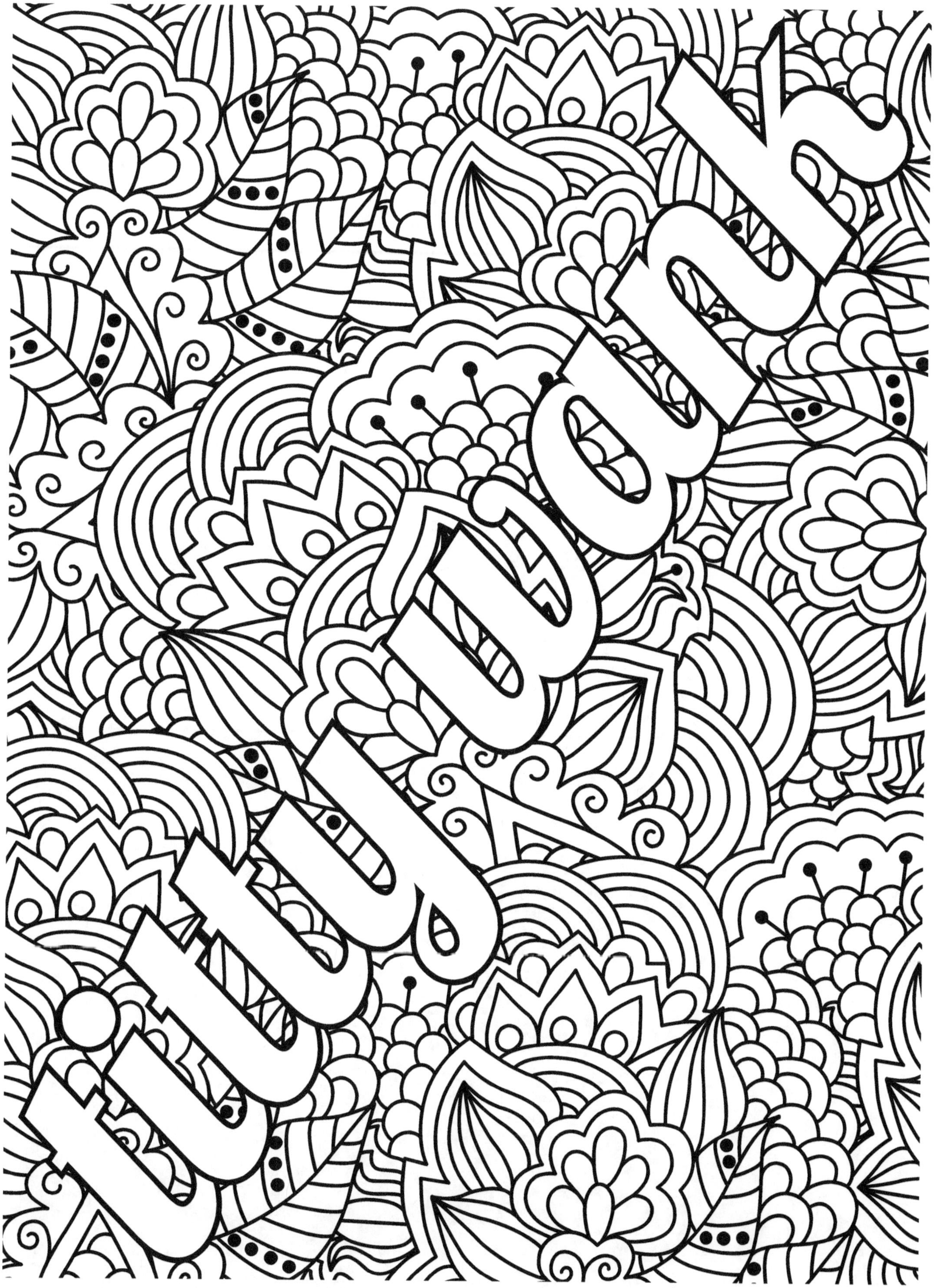
tittywank

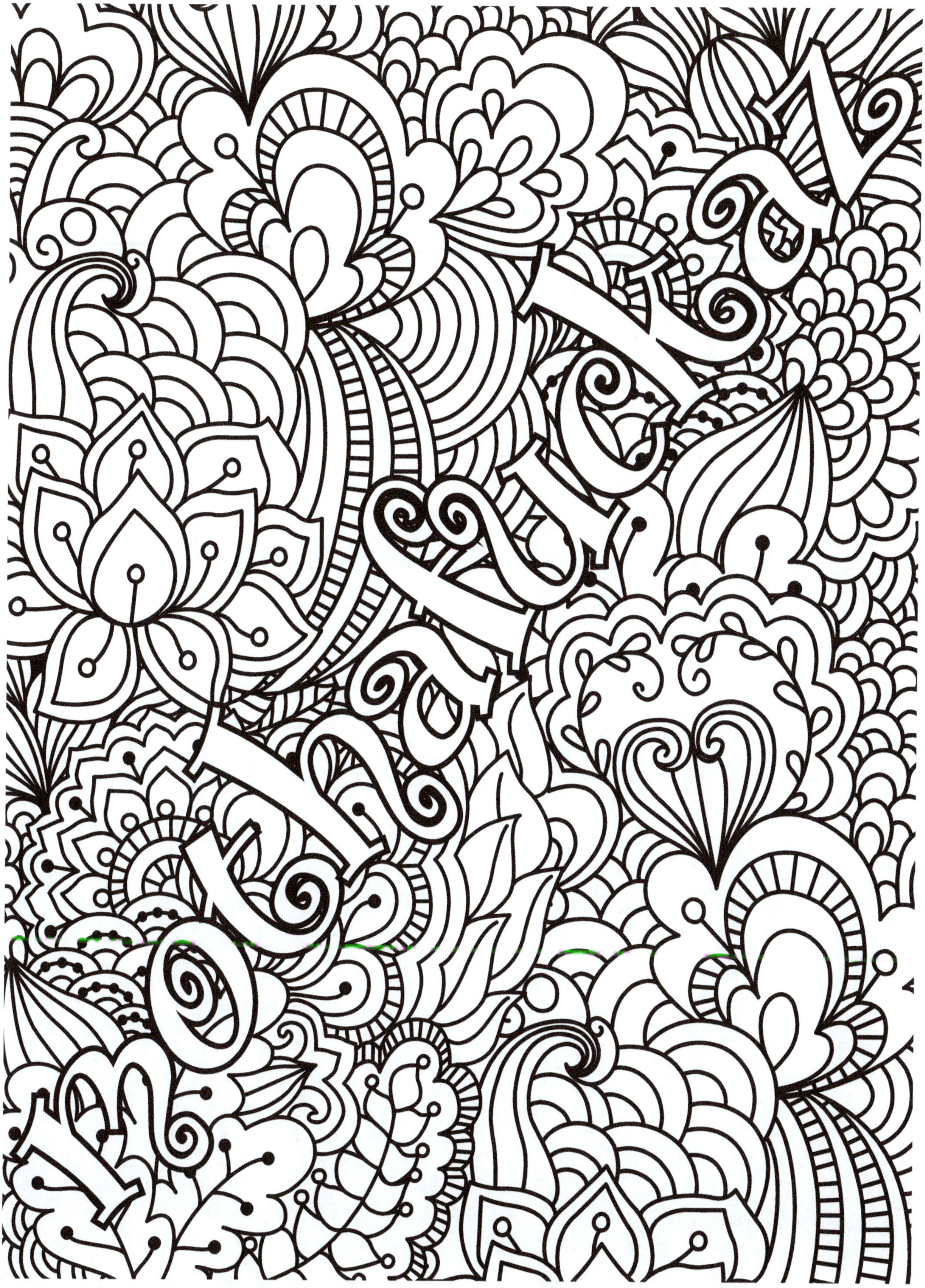

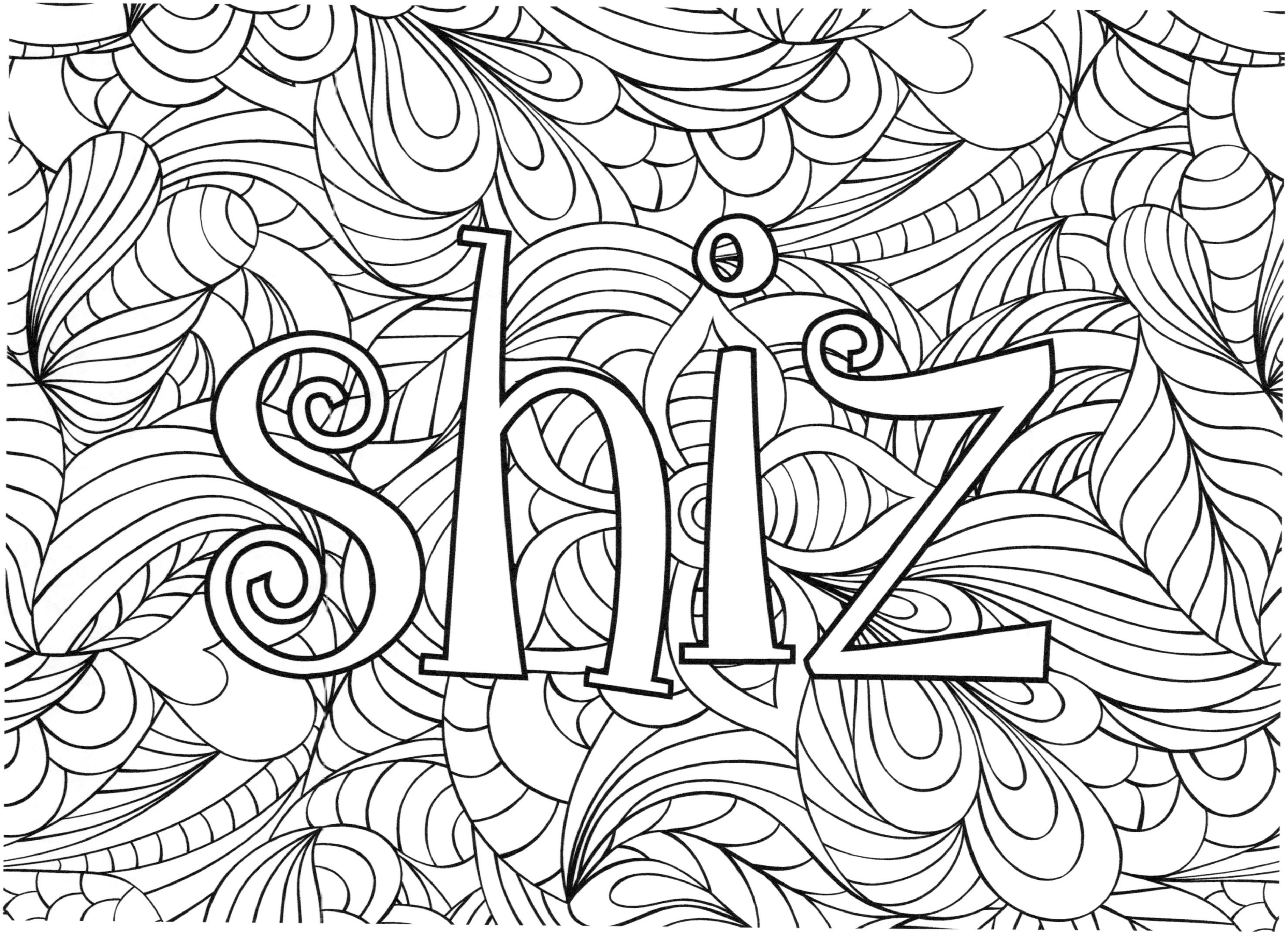
shiz

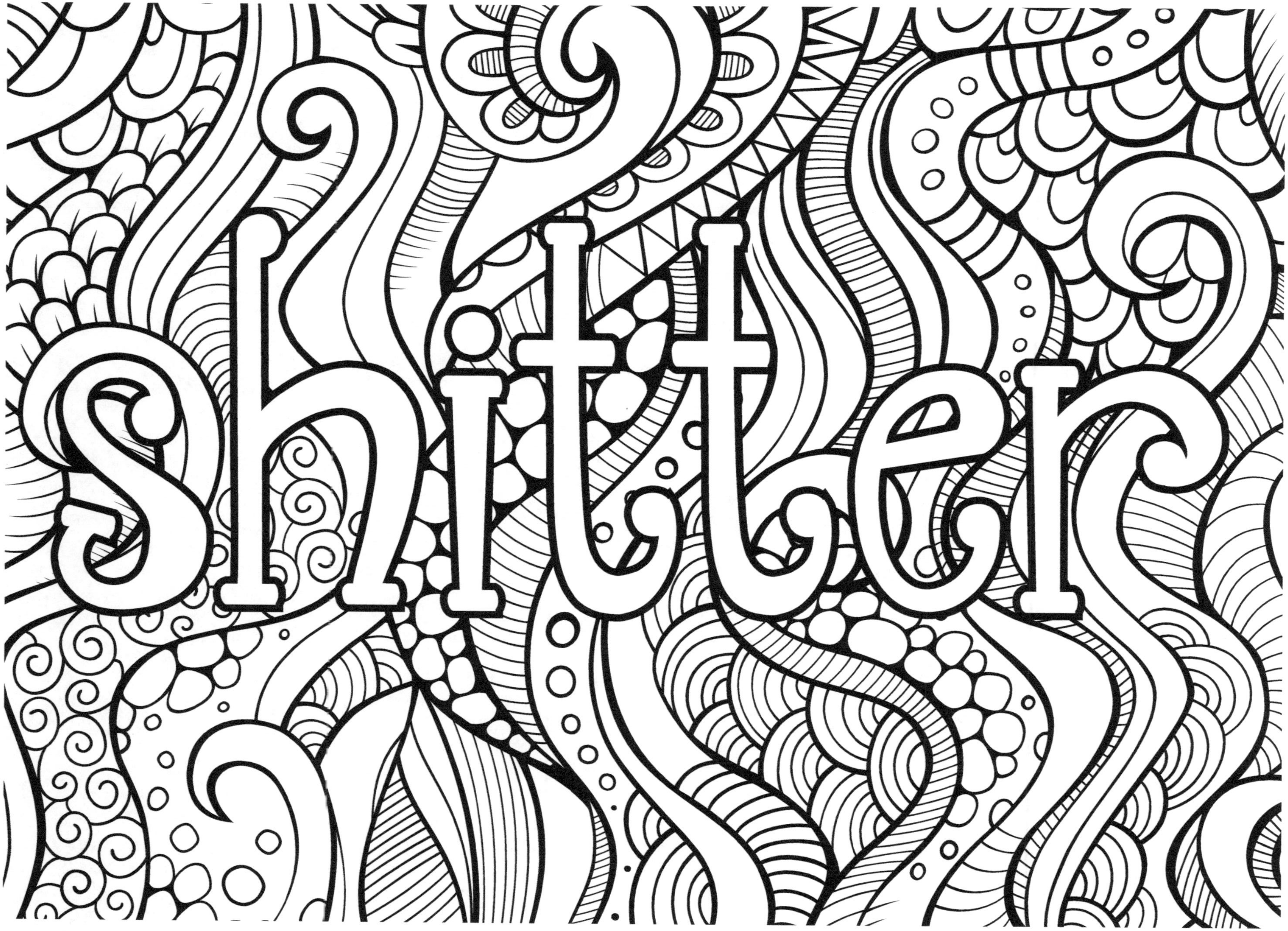
shitter

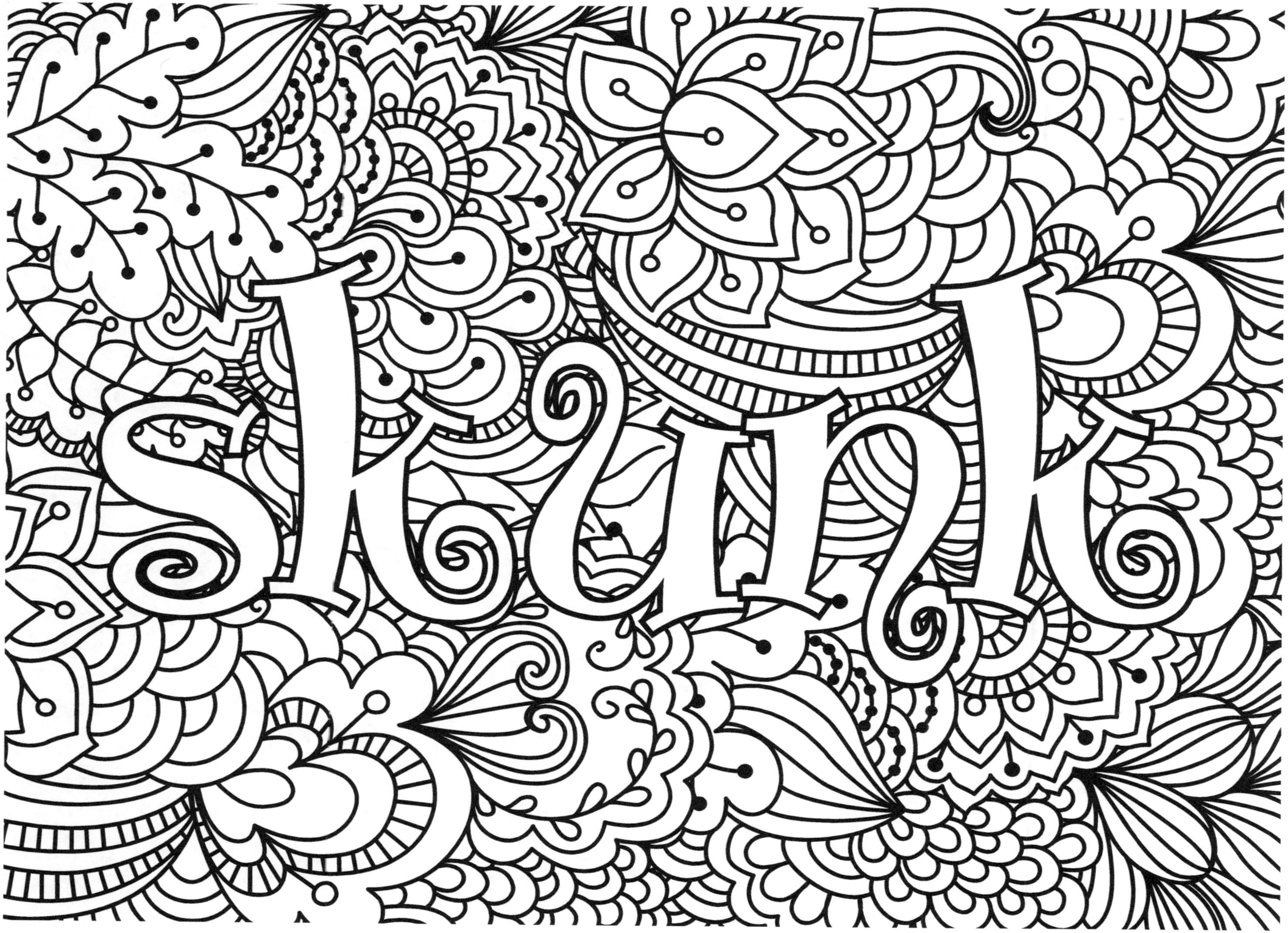
skunk

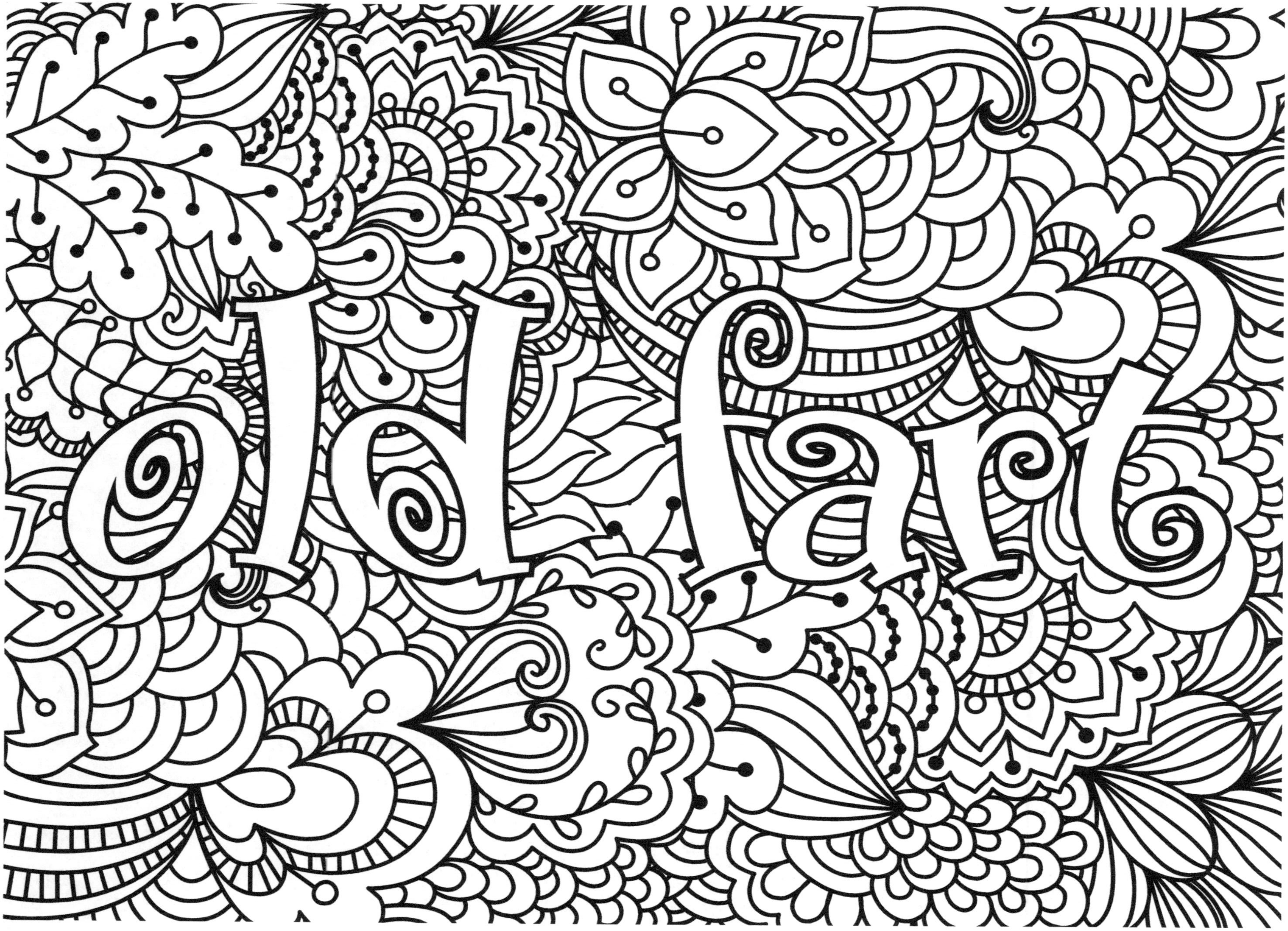
old fart

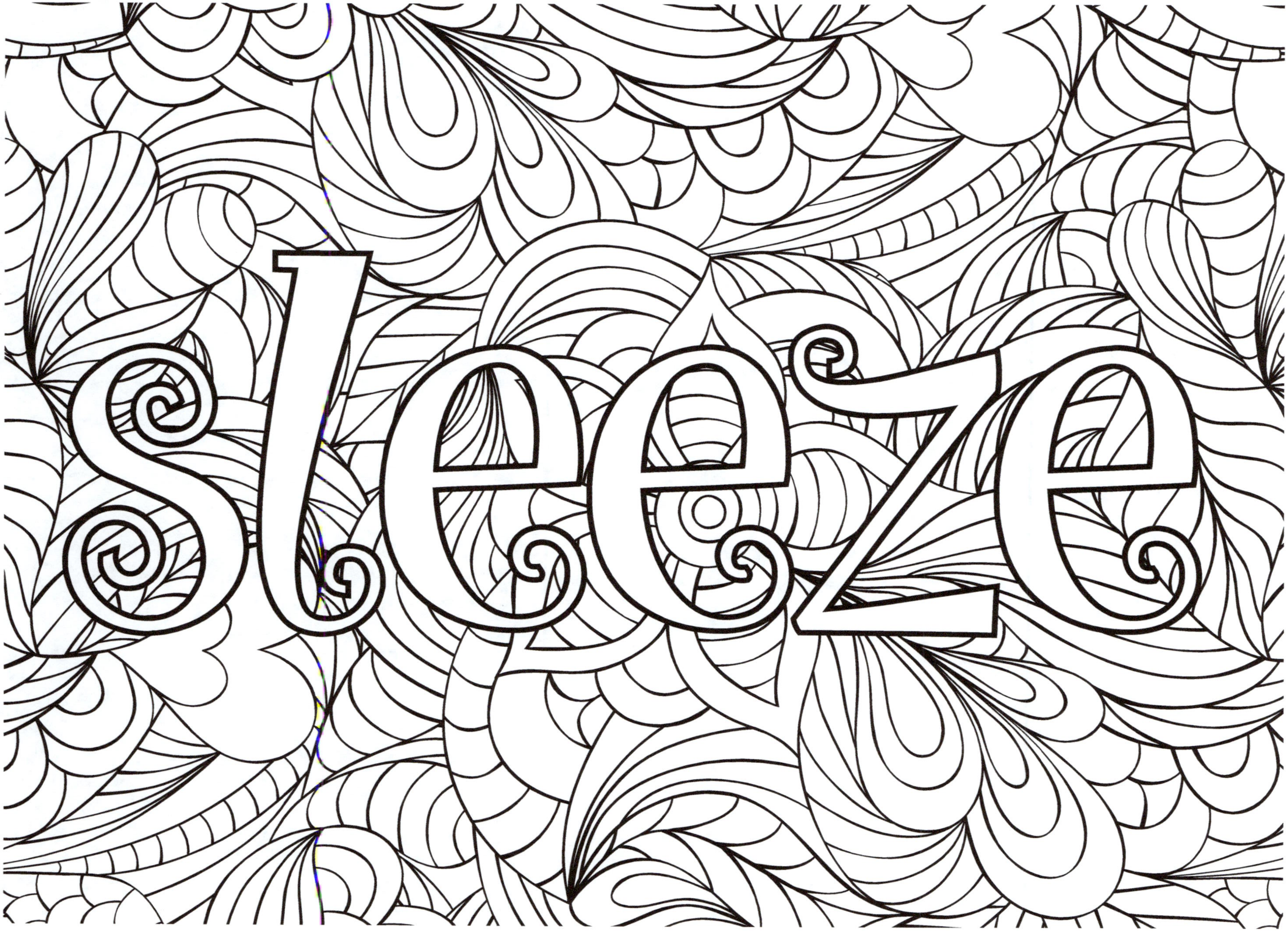
sleeze

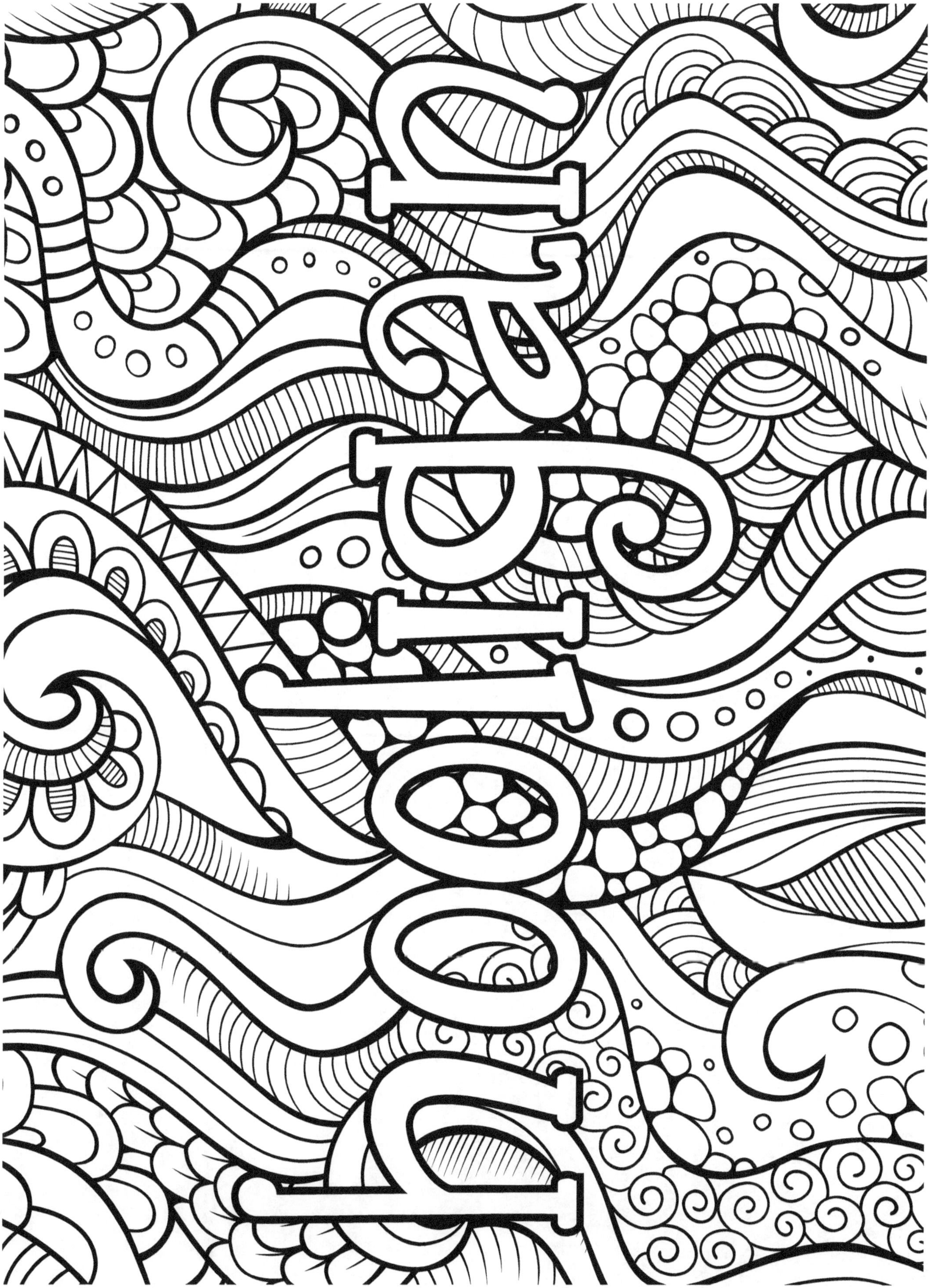
happy

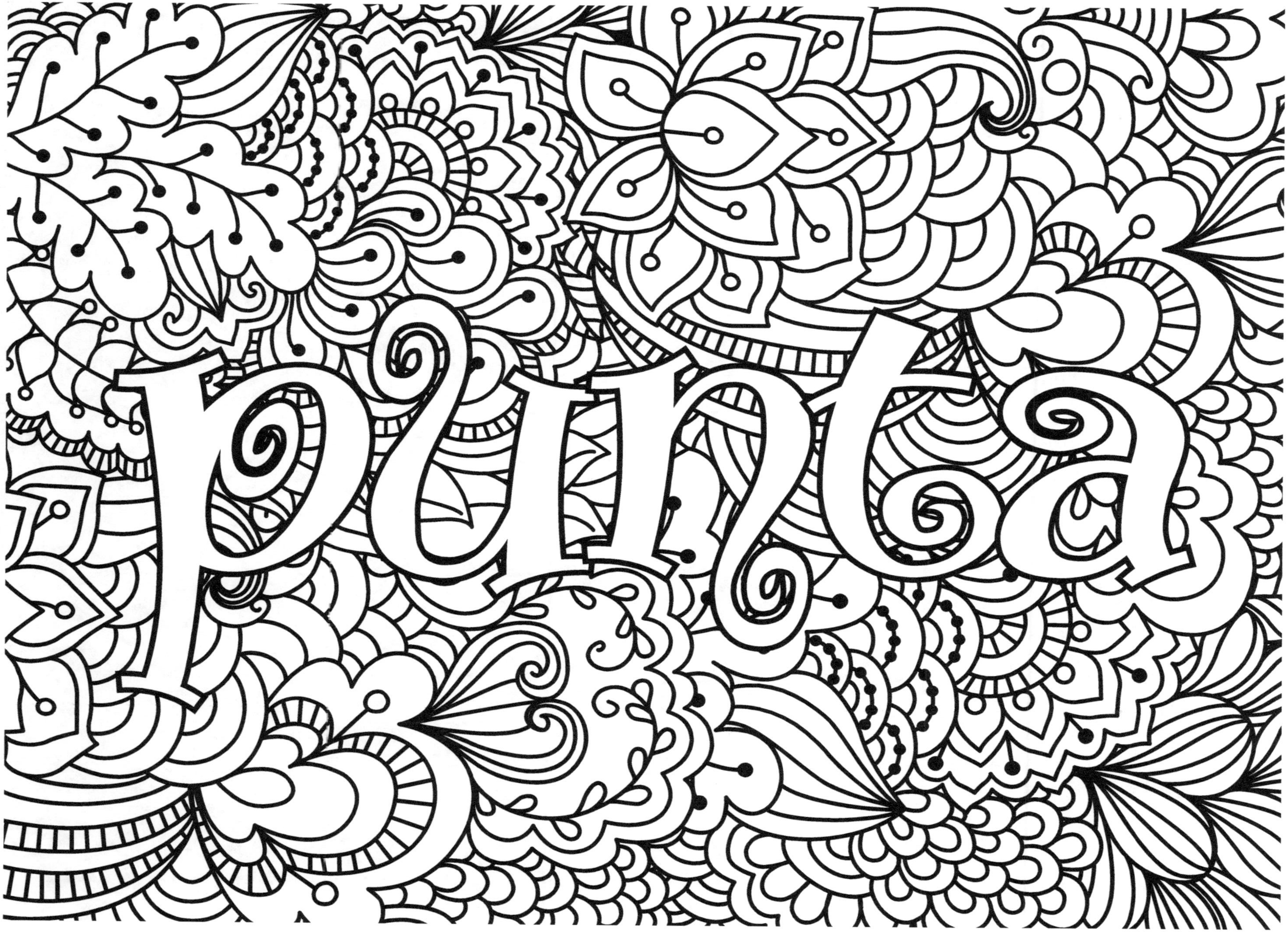
punta

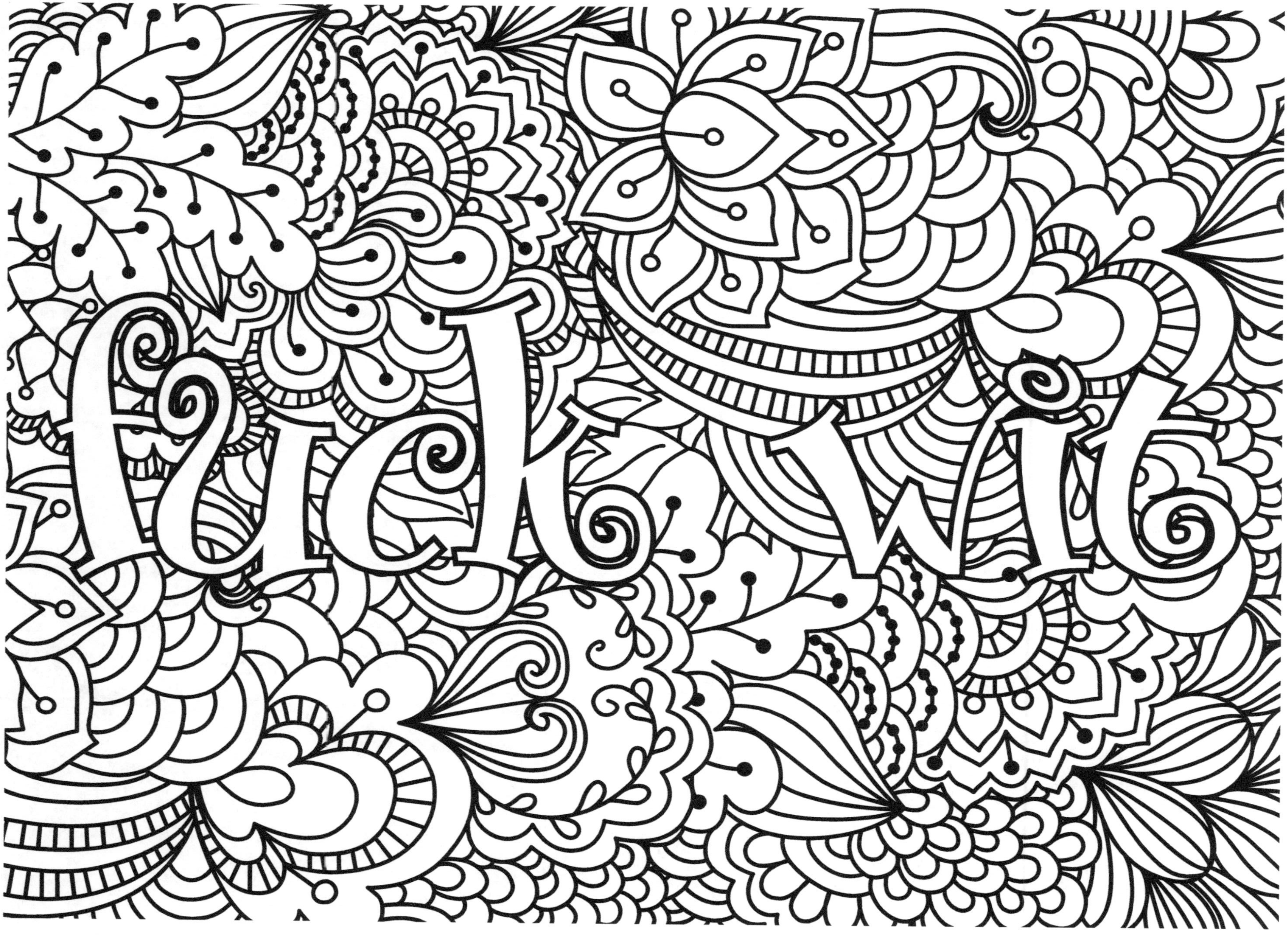
fuckwit

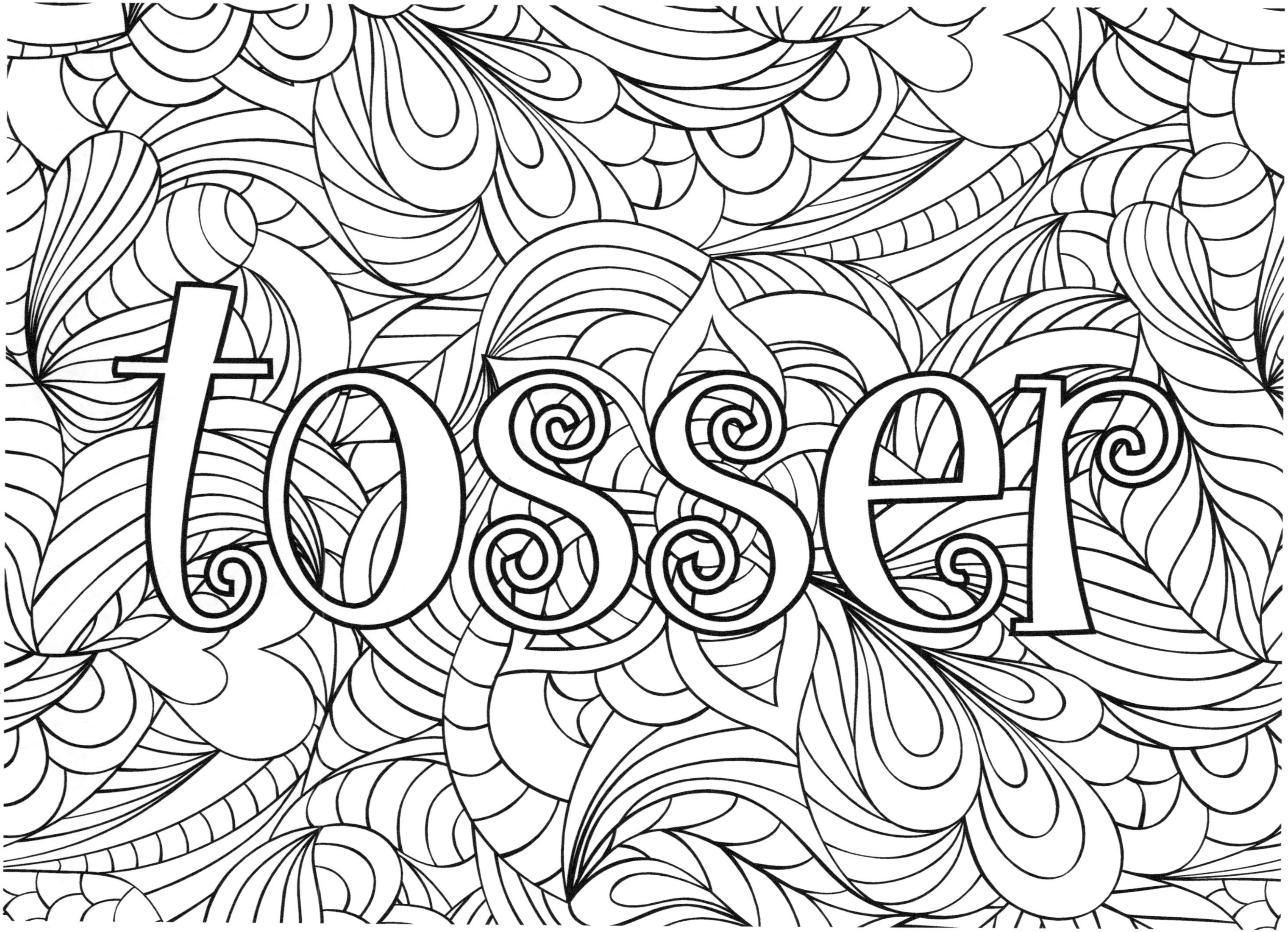
tosser

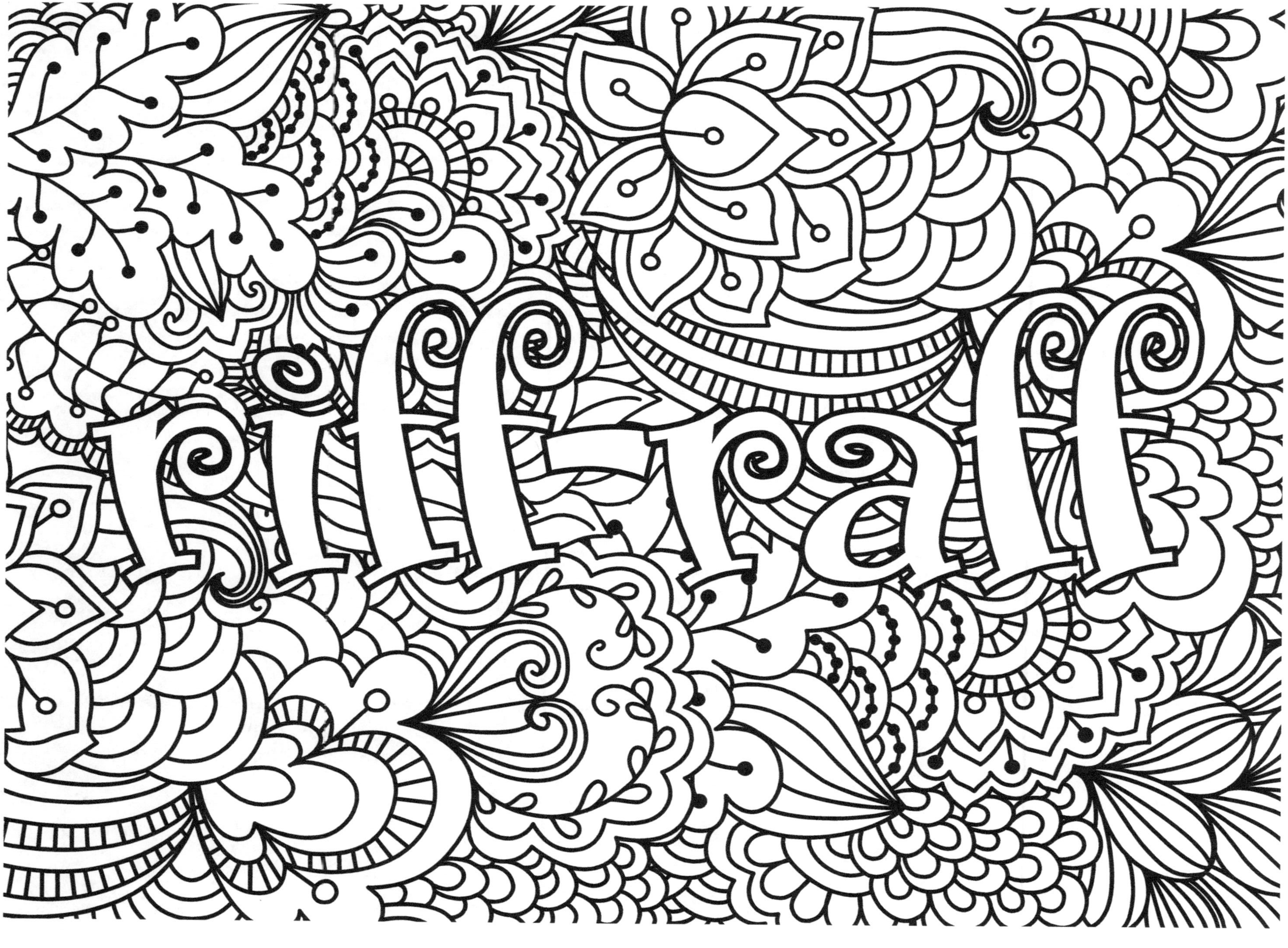
riff-raff

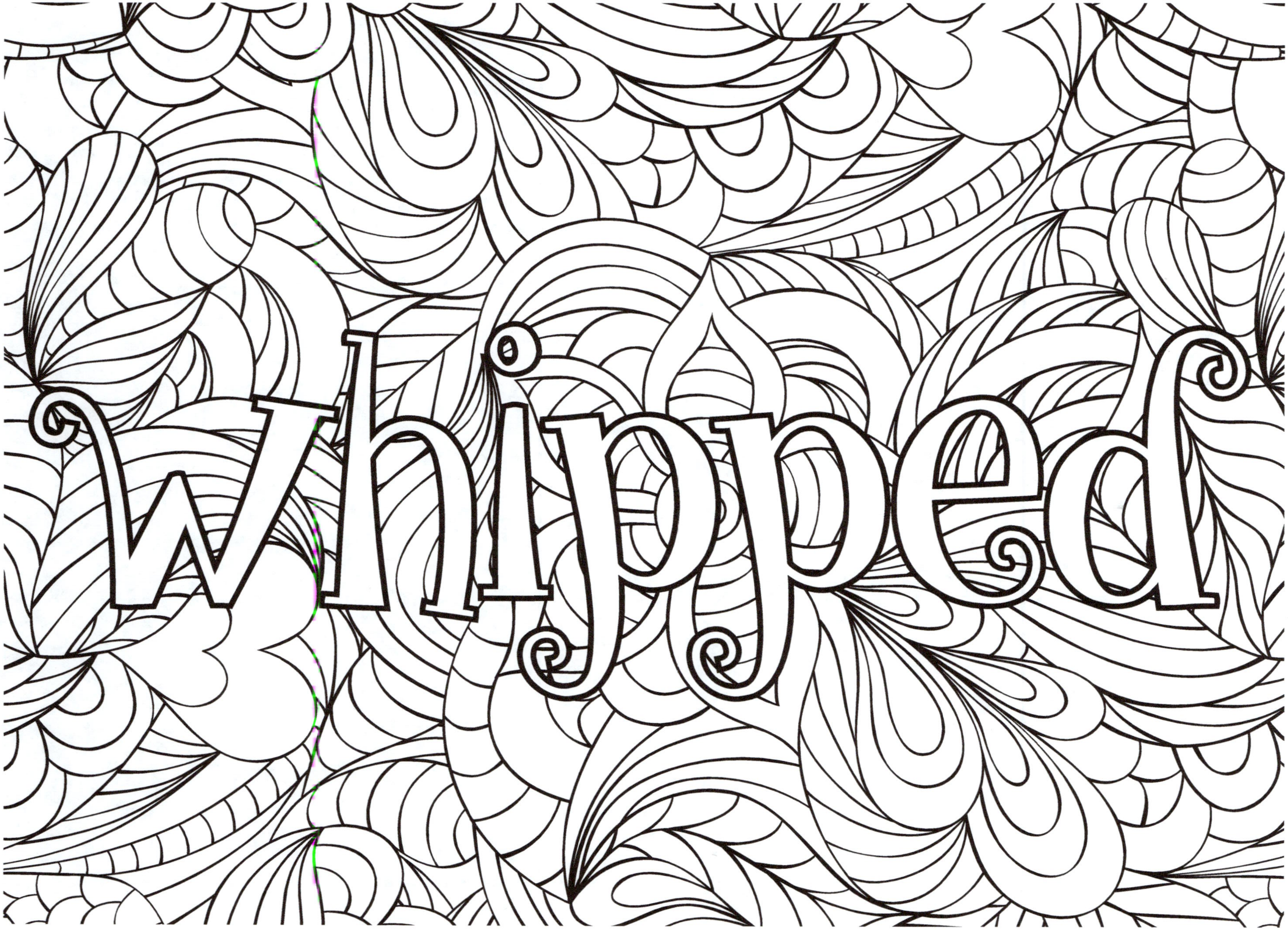
Whipped

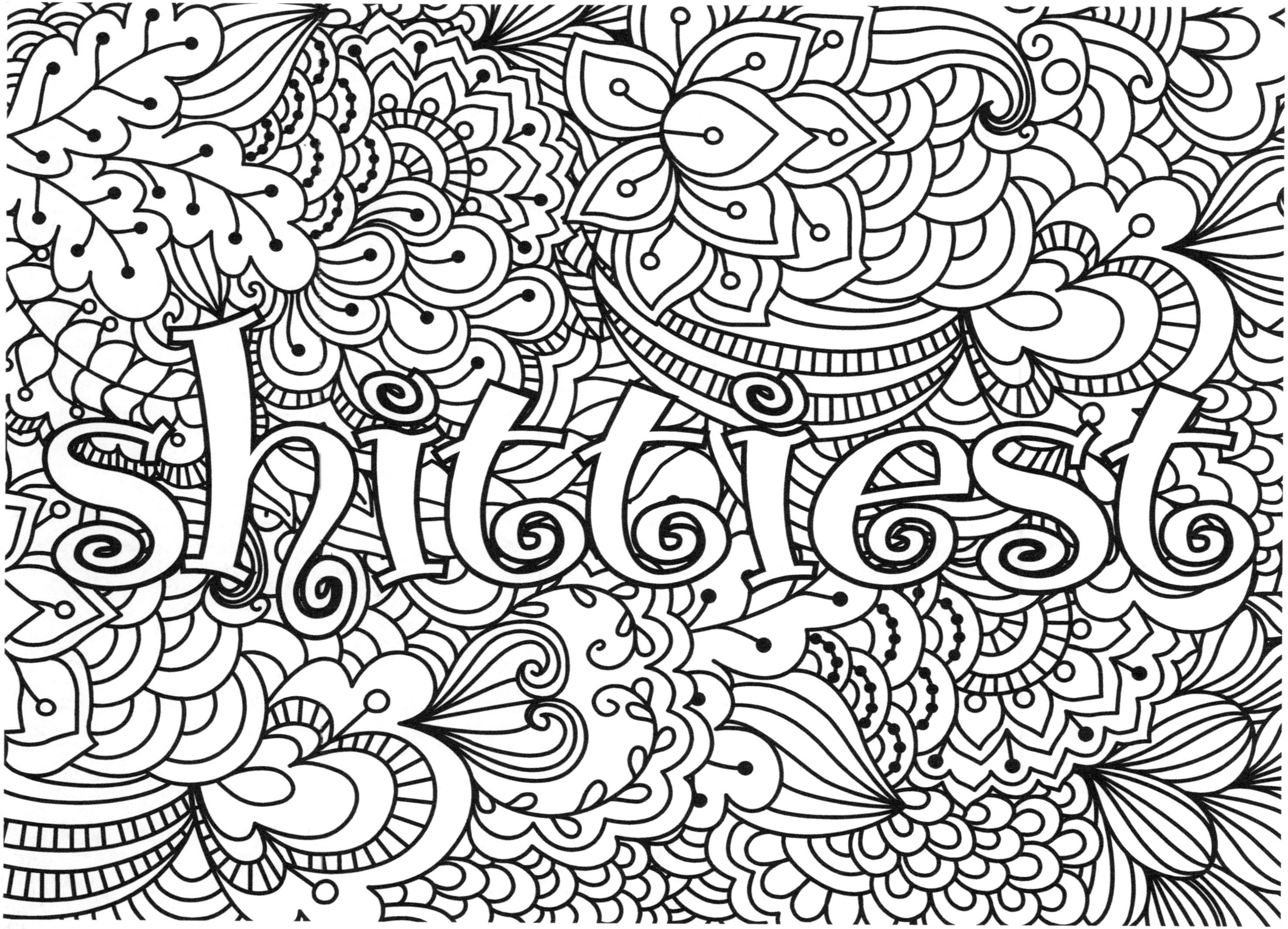
Shittiest

www.ingramcontent.com/pod-product-compliance
Lightning Source LLC
Chambersburg PA
CBHW080707190526
45169CB00006B/2278
* 9 7 8 1 5 3 2 7 6 4 8 6 8 *